WOMEN WARLORDS

AN ILLUSTRATED MILITARY
HISTORY OF FEMALE WARRIORS

TIM NEWARK

BLANDFORD

To Judy Chicago's Dinner Party

First published in the UK 1989 by **Blandford**, an imprint of Cassell
Villiers House, 41/47 Strand, London WC2N 5JE

This paperback edition published 1991

Distributed in the United States by
Sterling Publishing Co, Inc,
387 Park Avenue South, New York, NY 10016–8810

Distributed in Australia by
Capricorn Link (Australia) Pty Ltd
PO Box 665, Lane Cove, NSW 2066

British Library Cataloguing in Publication Data

Newark, Tim
    Women warlords: an illustrated military
history of ancient and medieval female
warriors.
    1. Women and war—History   2. Military
history, Ancient   3. Military history,
Medieval
I. Title   II. McBride, Angus
909.07   D25.5

ISBN 0 7137 2262 2

Typeset
by Graphicraft Hong Kong
Printed and bound in Great Britain
by The Bath Press

Contents

Preface

There have been occasions when women have assumed power on the death of their husbands. Many more have been content to wield influence behind the scenes, becoming formidable power-brokers for their husbands and children. All have maintained substantial private armies for the occasions when reasoned politics break down into open conflict. But few have emerged on to the battlefield to lead warriors in campaigns of aggression against other rulers. This book is about some of those women warlords.

Tim Newark
London

The True Amazons

Sometime before 1000 BC, a Greek adventurer sailed into the Black Sea. His name was Heracles and he landed at the mouth of the River Thermodon in northern Turkey. His warriors assembled on shore, setting up camp near the city of Themiscyra. Within its walls lived Hippolyte, Queen of the Amazons. Heracles sent an envoy to the Amazon queen, demanding the girdle she wore around her waist. It was his Ninth Labour. Hippolyte refused and her warriors, all women, rode out to confront Heracles and his men. As each side faced the other on the plains of Themiscyra, their champions advanced on foot to begin the battle in single combat.

Heracles wore no armour but a lion-skin, its paws tied around his neck and his head projecting through the mouth of the dead lion. He carried no shield and wielded only a bronze single-edged sword. From the ranks of the Amazons, a woman stepped forward, called Aella. Her name meant 'whirlwind' and she, too, wore no armour, carrying only a round shield, spear and sword. The two warriors followed each other's movements, jabbing their weapons in the air, carefully noting any weakness in the other's stance, any loss of nerve. Shuffling sideways in the dust, they circled each other. Their followers shouted words of encouragement and insult. Abruptly, Aella judged the moment had come. Her right arm stretched backwards and snapped forward, hurling her spear at the man before her. Heracles crouched against the ground. The spear clattered behind him. He sprang up towards the woman, delivering a mighty blow to her head. His men cheered triumphantly.

Several more women emerged from the Amazon army, each one a renowned champion. Heracles defeated them all. Finally, it was the turn of Melanippe, commander of the Amazon warriors. She wore a glittering breastplate, helmet and greaves, but even these were no protection against the fighting fury of the Greek hero. She too was felled and the Greek army rushed on the Amazons and defeated them. Heracles won the girdle of Hippolyte and sailed back to Mycenae. The Amazons were furious. They were a proud race and had conquered many peoples in the past. To avenge

9

this insult, they travelled to the land of the Scythians, along the northern coast of the Black Sea, and joined with them in an invasion of Greece.

The allied army of Amazons and Scythians advanced around the coast of the Black Sea, through Thrace into Attica. Outside Athens, they set up camp and demanded battle with Theseus, one of the leading Greek warriors to accompany Heracles on his expedition against them. Oreithyia, the Amazon commander, sent a contingent of warriors to the Peloponnese to prevent any reinforcements reaching the Athenians. After hesitation and delay on both sides, Theseus finally agreed to confront the invasion force. The Amazon-Scythian army gathered between what became called the Amazonium and the Pynx Hill. They were essentially an army of horse-warriors and fought as the Scythians fought: shooting bows from horseback, wielding lances, swords, and axes in close combat. They wore tight-fitting trousers and their horses were adorned with antler head-dresses of gold and bronze.

Theseus opened the battle. His Athenian right wing marched down from the Museum Hill and set upon the Amazon left wing. The women warriors surged forward on their horses and pelted the Greeks with arrows, breaking their lines, forcing them back as far as the Shrine of Eumenides. The Athenian left wing remained firm, allowing the whooping bands of female horse-warriors to pass by them, pursuing their routed comrades. Theseus then led them forward from the Palladium, Mount Ardettus, and the

Heracles delivering the death-blow to Hippolyte, Queen of the Amazons. From a Greek red-figure drinking-cup of the late sixth century BC. Hippolyte wears Greek-style armour typical of early Greek representations of Amazons.

Lyceum towards the Amazon right wing. The two forces bitterly contested the land, Amazon axe smashing against Greek shield, swords and spears breaking upon each other. At Theseus' side fought Antiope, an Amazon warrior Theseus had kidnapped, but who now was his wife and fought against her own people. In the fierce hand-to-hand combat, she fell dead to an Amazon javelin. Theseus increased the vigour of the Athenian attack and eventually the Amazons broke, falling back on their camp.

By the end of the campaign, Theseus expelled the Amazons from Greece. Rather than returning to their land around the River Thermodon, the Amazons remained with the Scythians in the land north of the Black Sea. This then is the mythical account of the war between the Greeks and Amazons—the Amazonomachy. It was a great victory for the Greeks: the first occasion they had defeated a foreign invader. For centuries, it remained one of the most popular subjects for Greek art, represented on hundreds of surviving vases. But what kind of victory was it? A triumph over a real or an imagined enemy?

To some, the war between the Amazons and the Greeks is symbolic of the struggle for domination between men and women. The Amazons were viewed by the Greeks as barbarians who had to be defeated to ensure the

Theseus battling with Amazons on an Athenian *dinos* of the mid-fifth century BC. Andromache, on her knees, carries both an axe and bow, weapons characteristic of the classical Amazons.

survival of a settled, civilised society. To that end, the Amazonomachy may represent prehistoric battles around the Mediterranean between matriarchies and patriarchies with the male-dominated, non-nomadic societies eventually winning through. But it would be wrong to dismiss the Amazons as a mythical device with no basis in recorded history. There is a considerable body of evidence suggesting that the Amazons were true women warriors living sometime in the ancient world.

The earliest literary evidence of the Amazons occurs in Homer's *Iliad*. In his eighth-century BC account of a Mycenean war against Troy, Homer describes the Amazons as a fantastic enemy of the hero, Bellerophon, who destroyed them alongside the ferocious Chimera, part lion, goat and serpent. This reference is matched by Hesiod, writing a little later, who tells of Heracles fighting against the Amazons as he searches for the finest horses in Asia. This is certainly the stuff of court entertainment, tales of heroes battling against monsters designed to please a male Greek warlord, and yet, in Hesiod's reference we already have a clue to the reality of the Amazons. They live in a land of fine horses in Asia. This is expanded upon by Hippocrates in the fifth century BC, who specifically identifies the women warriors with the Sarmatians living north of the Black Sea, around the Sea of Azov.

'There is a Scythian race,' wrote Hippocrates, 'dwelling around Lake Maeotis [the Sea of Azov] which differs from other races. Their name is Sauromatae [Greek for Sarmatians]. Their women ride, shoot, and throw javelins while mounted. They remain virgins until they have killed three of their enemies and only then may they marry once they have performed the traditional sacred rites. A woman who takes a husband may no longer ride unless she has to at times of war. They have no right breast because when they are babies, their mothers apply a red-hot bronze instrument to the right breast and cauterise it, so its growth is arrested and all its strength and bulk are diverted to the right shoulder and arm.'

In this passage, we have the classic motif of the Amazon legend. Their right breast is stunted at birth. It is from this that they were supposed to derive their name: *a mazos* being Greek for 'without a breast'. This detail is repeated by later historians who explain that the breast was removed to facilitate the drawing of a bow. There is, of course, no real physical advantage to be gained from this and the only possible explanation, if it were true, is that it was a form of ritual mutilation. A more plausible suggestion is that the name Amazon is derived from an Armenian word meaning 'moon-women' and refers to Asian priestesses, south of the Caucasian Mountains, who worshipped a moon goddess. In their early travels, Greeks may have confused representations of these priestesses with accounts of real women warriors north of the Caucasian Mountains. It was probably because of this linguistic confusion that many ancient writers believed the home of the Amazons lay in the plains of Themiscyra along the southern Black Sea coast of Turkey, west of Armenia.

Amazon in part-Scythian, part-Oriental clothes on a Greek neck-amphora. By the mid-fifth century BC, true reports of Sarmatian Amazons may have encouraged Greek artists to represent them in more realistic Asian garb.

Herodotus, also writing in the fifth century BC, tried to explain the contradiction between the mythical homeland of the Amazons and true reports of Sarmatian women warriors from the northern shores of the Black Sea. With a story born from the legendary exploits of Heracles, he relates that after their victory against the Amazons of Themiscyra, the Greeks set sail with several ships full of Amazon prisoners. Out on the Black Sea, the Amazons overcame the crews of the ships and killed them. Driven northwards by a storm, the Amazons found themselves near the shore of the Sea of Azov, in the realm of the Scythians. Dropping anchor, they explored the strange land and ambushed the first group of horsemen they met. Taking their horses, they then raided the territory of the Scythians. At first, the Scythians thought the invaders were men but as they clashed with them, they learnt their true identity. Rather than carrying on a war against them, the Scythians were impressed by the valour of the women and encouraged their young men to pursue them, for they wanted children by them.

The young Scythians knew the Amazons could never be overcome by force, so they followed them, avoiding any conflict. If the Amazons chased them, they fled before them. If the Amazons retreated, then the Scythians moved their camps closer to them. Eventually, the Amazons could see the young men meant them no harm and they came together, accepting each other as sexual partners. Children were born to them and the Scythian men lived on the steppes in the Amazon camps. But the men grew home-sick.

'We have parents and possessions,' they told the Amazons. 'Let us return home and we will still have you, and no others, for our wives.'

'We cannot dwell in your society, with your women,' the Amazons replied. 'For we do not share the same customs. We shoot with the bow, throw the javelin, and ride. Your women do none of these things, but live in wagons and work at women's crafts and never go hunting. We could never accept that. If you wish to live with us as man and wife then go to your parents, demand your share of their possessions, and return to us so that we can live by ourselves.'

The Scythians agreed and returned to the Amazons with their possessions. But the Amazons were still not happy.

'We are filled with fear and dread,' they told their men. 'How can we live in this land now that we have deprived you of your parents. We have done too much harm to you. If you think it right that we should live together then we must move away from this land across the River Don.'

To this, the Scythian men also agreed and joined the Amazons in a journey north-eastwards from the Sea of Azov to the land where, according to Herodotus, they lived in the fifth century BC. The Greek historian went on to say that the descendants of this coupling were the Sarmatians who continued the ancient tradition of the Amazons. 'Their women go hunting with or without their men,' he says. 'They go to war and wear the same dress as the men. In regard to marriage, it is the custom that no virgin weds

Scythian-Sarmatian horse head-dress surmounted with head of horned lion-griffin, made of leather, felt, copper and gilt hair. From Pazirik in western Siberia, late fifth century BC, now in the Hermitage, Leningrad.

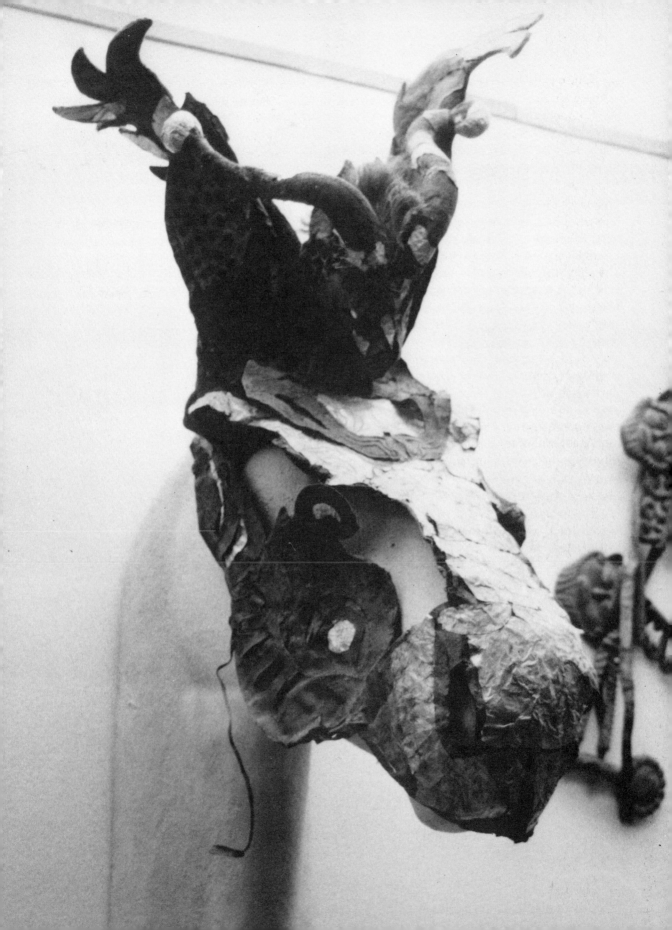

till she has slain a man of the enemy and because of this some of them grow old and die unmarried.' With this information, similar to that of Hippocrates, Herodotus concludes his origin of the Sarmatian Amazons. Through combining fable with actual observation, Herodotus clearly removes the Amazons from their mythical homeland south of the Black Sea to their true location along the northern coast.

In later centuries, ancient historians tried to identify the Amazons directly with the Scythians. Diodorus of Sicily, in the first century BC, explained that during the early history of the Scythians, there was a period of revolutions, 'in which the sovereigns were women endowed with exceptional valour'. He then identifies these women rulers with those living along the Thermodon in northern Turkey, but makes no effort to explain how they got there from Scythia. Pompeius Trogus, also in the first century BC, identified the Amazons with the Scythians, but came up with an ingenious explanation for their presence south of the Black Sea. At the period of their greatest conquests, two Scythian princes founded a colony at the mouth of the River Thermodon. Initially, they successfully raided their neighbours, but the native people united and ambushed them, completely destroying all the Scythian warriors. Their wives, living in Themiscyra with no one to defend them, were forced to take to arms. Several times, they fought off the natives. Determined to stay within their colony, they refused any possibility of intermarriage with their neighbours, saying it would be slavery, not matrimony. They then established a government without men, putting to death any men that had survived the destruction of their male warriors.

In both these later accounts of the Amazons, a great deal of mythologising is added to their description. Not only do they now live in a mythical land around the Thermodon, but they have also ceased to be real women in equal partnership with their men. They have become tyrannical warlords, dominating the men around them. Diodorus gives a classic description: 'To their men, the Amazon Queen assigned the spinning of wool and other domestic duties as belong to women. Laws were established in which she led women to war, but the men were confined to humiliation and slavery. As for their children, they mutilated the legs and arms of the males so they could not fight.' Other later historians seized upon these tales to continue the portrayal of the Amazons as men-hating tyrants—a warning to men of the folly of allowing women any power at all.

Such an attitude is clearly intended to foster male prejudices at the height of Roman imperialism, by which time the true Sarmatian Amazons may well have disappeared. Indeed, in his first-century AD *Geography*, Strabo doubts whether they ever really existed. 'As regards the Amazons,' he writes, 'the same stories are told now as in early times, even though they are beyond belief. For instance, who could believe that an army of women, or a city, or a tribe, could ever be organised without men, and not only be organised, but overpower the peoples near them and even send an expedition across

16

the sea as far as Attica? For this is the same as saying that the men of those times were women and that the women were men.' Clearly, there has been a major change in male attitudes since the early literate Greeks writing in the fifth century BC and those Romanised Greeks of the first century BC. To the early Greek historians, the Amazons were a real people living along the north-eastern coast of the Black Sea, pursuing a unique form of sexual equality. To later historians, they were a mythical race, serving only as an amusing warning to men. But what other evidence is there to reinforce the reports of the early Greeks that the Amazons actually existed?

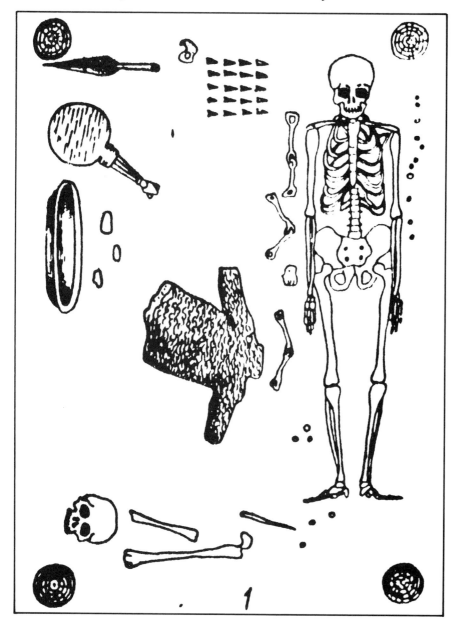

Ukrainian barrow burial containing mail shirt, lance, arrow heads and bronze mirror. Burials similar to these have been ascribed to Sarmatian Amazons. Drawn after Chernenko.

In the 1950s and 1960s, Soviet archaeologists made a series of remarkable discoveries. At the base of a burial shaft near the River Molochnaya on the north-west coast of the Sea of Azov, 220 miles (350 km) east of Odessa, lay the skeleton of a young woman. Beside her were the usual signs of a privileged female background: a bronze mirror, a necklace of glass beads, silver, bronze and glass bracelets, and a Greek amphora from across the Black Sea. But, in addition to these luxuries, two iron lance blades were found close to her skull. A quiver of 20 arrows and a suit of iron-scale armour lay next to her. She was a true Amazon. A woman warrior living sometime in the fourth or third centuries BC and belonging to the people known as Sarmatians. The discovery was not isolated. Within a barrow grave at Kut, sunk within the steppes west of the River Dnieper, a female skeleton of the same period was found surrounded by a bronze mirror, bronze ear-rings, a glass-bead necklace, an iron sword and the remains of a quiver with 36 arrows. At Zemo-Avchala, near Tbilisi in Georgia, in the northern foothills of the Caucasian Mountains, Soviet farmers stumbled upon a grave containing a woman buried in a crouching position, surrounded by weapons. At Kholodnyi Yar on the Tjasmin, a female skeleton lay with a bronze mirror and iron lance-heads at her side and the skeleton of an attendant at her feet. There have been several other such finds. All dating from the fourth and third centuries BC and all identified as belonging to the Sarmatian culture. This is the archaeological evidence of the twentieth century proving the truth of literary accounts 2,500 years ago.

So, as the Sarmatian Amazons really existed, what kind of people were they? According to further archaeological evidence, the Sarmatians were an Indo-European people whose territory stretched from the Ukraine to Kazakhstan, beyond the Caspian Sea. The land they inhabited was primarily steppe, thousands of kilometres of treeless grassland bordered by Siberian forest in the north and Central Asian desert in the south. In the western region, the Caucasus Mountains formed a barrier between the Sarmatians and the Persian Empire. Naturally, they were nomads, following a regular cycle of grazing horses and cattle, hunting fish and game. Sometimes drought could disrupt their usual round of pastures and they would be forced to raid neighbouring people or settled city communities. The Sarmatians were excellent horse-warriors, capable of shooting powerful bows from the back of their steppe ponies and closing with lance and long cavalry swords. It is indicative of this background that many classic Amazon names derive from Greek horse phrases: Melanippe (black mare); Hippolyte (stampeding horse); Alcippe (powerful mare).

Within this steppe society, it appears from all the literary evidence that women enjoyed a greater degree of equality and power than among other neighbouring cultures. Among the Scythians, for example, all women lived a life of complete Asiatic seclusion. The Scythians were polygamists, their sons often inheriting their father's wives. In contrast, at Pazirik in

Sarmatian horseman in scale armour similar to that worn by Sarmatian Amazons. Marble stele found at Tanais in the Ukraine and now in the Hermitage, Leningrad. (*Overleaf*)

19

Kazakhstan, single women have been found sharing the coffins of their Sarmatian husbands. This suggests that the Sarmatians were monogamous and even though married Sarmatian women had to devote themselves to raising a family, the marriage was more a partnership in which the woman was a wife rather than a concubine or servant. And, of course, until the point of marriage, Sarmatian girls were able to hunt and fight alongside boys. It may be true that some women never married, preferring to compete within the Sarmatian hierachy and rise to a position of power in the tribe. This would explain the presence of single armed women in graves usually associated with tribal chieftains. That women enjoyed an unusually active role in Sarmatian society may also stem from their influence as priestesses. Low stone tables, thought to be altars, have been discovered in Sarmatian female graves in the southern Urals and Kazakhstan.

In the sixth and fifth centuries BC, the western Sarmatians, living between the Rivers Don and Volga, were very much under the domination of the Scythians. At the height of their power, the Scythians were a formidable steppe confederacy, benefiting greatly from their contacts across the Black Sea with both Greek and Persian civilisations, and sometimes extending their martial rule over parts of Europe and the Near East. Before these mighty horsemen, it is likely that the western Sarmatians paid tribute and were influenced by their culture. It is not surprising that ancient historians confused the early Sarmatians with the Scythians. It is also not surprising that Sarmatian Amazon warriors should fight alongside the Scythians in their raids against Europe and Asia. This may go some way to explaining the legendary invasion of Greece against Theseus. Certainly, from the late sixth century BC onwards, Greek vases cease to portray the Amazons as simply women in Greek armour, but paint them as Scythians in trousers and riding horses, shooting bows. This suggests increased Greek reports of true Sarmatian Amazons riding with Scythians.

One of the greatest contests to the power of the Scythians occurred in the sixth century BC when the Persians, under Darius the Great, invaded their land. It is the first instance of an historically true campaign in which the Sarmatian Amazons are said to have played a key role. Around 512 BC, the Persian emperor crossed the Bosporus and invaded Europe. He planned to conquer Greece, but first he had to secure the northern Balkans against the Scythians around the Black Sea. He also wished to deny the Greeks wood from Thrace and grain from the Ukraine. Advancing through Thrace, he reached the Danube with a huge army numbering some 700,000, according to Herodotus, though probably only a tenth of that. On the banks of the river, a wooden pontoon bridge was constructed to take the Persians on to Scythian territory. Darius left a rearguard of Ionian Greeks to protect it, giving them a rope tied with 60 knots. Each day Darius was away fighting the Scythians, the Ionians were ordered to untie a knot on the rope. If Darius had not returned by the end of the 60 knots, then the Ionians were to break up the bridge and sail home.

ΤΡΥΦΩΝΙ
ΝΑ ΡΟΜΕΝΟΥΑΝΕ

21

As the Persians stepped on Scythian territory, the Scythian rulers realised the magnitude of the Persian threat. Their messengers reported the vast columns of men and equipment, forcing the Scythians to admit they could never battle them alone. They called upon neighbouring peoples to unite against the Persians. Several tribes refused, saying it was the Scythians who had provoked the Persians and they had nothing to fear. But the Sarmatians understood the sense of a united front and placed themselves at the service of the Scythians. Many Amazons rode in the ranks of Sarmatians and possibly there were women commanders. Herodotus tells us that Tomyris, Queen of the Massagetae in Central Asia in the sixth century, defeated a Persian army led by Cyrus and personally cut off the head of the emperor. The Persians had much to fear from the Amazons.

Employing the classic strategy of the Russian steppes, the Scythians decided to retreat before Darius, driving off cattle, poisoning wells, burning grass. The Scythian army was divided: the first half led by King Scopasis included the Sarmatians; the second, commanded by Kings Idanthyrsus and Taxacis, incorporated the allied steppe tribes of the Geloni and Budini. Scopasis withdrew eastwards, drawing the Persians towards the River Don and the land of the Sarmatians, north of the Sea of Azov. Idanthyrsus and the second contingent shadowed the Persians, preventing them from turning northwards, where the Scythians had sent their women, children and livestock. A small Scythian advance-guard was sent close to the enemy to tempt them ever onwards across the barren steppes. In the summer, the land north of the Black Sea swelters under the sun and the dark clouds rising from burning pasture-land profoundly reduced the morale of the Persians with each day's march eastwards. Back at the Ionian rearguard on the Danube, a third of the knots on Darius' rope had been untied. Darius was growing tired of the fruitless pursuit and sent a messenger to the Scythian King Idanthyrsus.

'Strange man,' he said, 'why do you always run away? You could choose to stand and fight if you consider yourself strong enough. But if you believe you are weak, then why not stop this running and make your submission to me, bringing me gifts of land and water?'

Sarmatian lance head and spear-head, fourth or third centuries BC. The Sarmatians were noted for their use of long, heavy lances, often wielded in both hands.

Scythian bronze mountain
goat decoration from horse
trappings, fifth century BC.
Found near Chigrin and now
in the Hermitage, Leningrad.

'I have never fled for fear of any man,' replied the Scythian. 'I do not flee from you now, but travel as I always do in peace. But if you wish to know why we do not fight with you, it is because we do not possess towns or farmlands that would force us to protect them. But if you do wish to battle with us, then seek our fathers' tombs for then you will find out whether we fight or not. Until then we shall not battle you.'

Instead of gifts, the Scythians sent groups of horsemen to harass the Persian lines of communication stretching back to the Danube. The Sarmatians and the Scythians under Scopasis rode to the Ionian rearguard and persuaded them to break up the bridge, but as soon as they went away, the Ionians broke their word. In the meantime, while the Persians searched for food on the steppes, they were attacked by Scythian horse-archers. The Persian cavalry fell back on to their infantry formations and the Scythians rode off rather than face them. Herodotus writes that the Persians were also saved by the presence of mules in their army, because the horses of the Scythians were apparently unused to the braying of the mules and were reluctant to approach them. Despite this unforeseen weapon, the Persians were shaken by the constant assault and Darius was fast losing interest in the entire campaign. At this point, the Scythian King Idanthyrsus sent an envoy to the Persian camp. The messenger delivered a bird, a mouse, a frog and five arrows. Were these the gifts of land and water that Darius had asked for? Maybe the Scythians too were suffering from the war across their land.

Darius asked his advisers how he should interpret the strange gifts. He thought they were symbols of surrender: the mouse representing the earth; the frog the water; the bird the horses of the Scythians; and the arrows their fighting power. But one of his advisers, Gobryas, was not so sure.

'Great emperor,' he explained, 'I believe the meaning of the gifts is not of surrender. The Scythians say that unless you become birds and fly up into the sky, or mice and hide in the earth, or frogs and leap into the lakes, you will be shot by these arrows and never return home.'

The Persian emperor could not win. As Darius prepared to lead his weary soldiers homewards, the steppe horsemen finally appeared in force on the low horizon. Their horse-archers dashed forward, followed by more heavily armoured Sarmatian and Scythian nobles. It seemed that the Scythians had at last agreed to a confrontation. Darius hurriedly ordered his warriors into their formations and awaited battle. As the two sides stood in line, a hare suddenly popped up and bounded across the plain. The Scythians and Sarmatians liked nothing better than a hunt. Despite being prepared for battle, they could not resist the tiny creature and a body of horsemen broke away from the Scythian army, chasing it wildly with whoops of excitement. Darius asked his advisers for an explanation of the sudden disintegration of the Scythian force. Once he heard the reason for it, he was greatly depressed.

'Do the Scythians regard us with such contempt? They have had nothing but sport with us.'

Sarmatian short sword,
fourth or third centuries BC.

Without waiting any further opportunity of battle, Darius ordered his men home. The Scythians, with their Sarmatian allies, had won. The steppes would remain free from the conquests of any sedentary empire, even that of the Romans. The campaign against the Persians reveals the essential strategy of all nomadic warfare. Amazons undoubtedly rode in the Scythian army and must have further struck fear into the Persians. During the next century, the Scythians continued to dominate the region north of the Black Sea, but their eastern neighbours, the Sarmatians, were also learning the special benefits to be won from trade connections across the water.

The fourth century BC saw a shift in power across the Eurasian steppes. The Massagetae of Central Asia expanded their influence over the Sarmatian tribes of Kazakhstan and took possession of the lower Volga region, north of the Caspian Sea. Around the east coast of the Sea of Azov, the Bosporan Greek trading kingdom remained vigorous. Pressed by the Massagetae to the east of them, the Sarmatians moved westwards across the River Don into the territory of the Scythians. In their western regions, bordering Thrace, the Scythians were still strong and defeated their Macedonian enemies, but in the east they gave way before the advance of the Sarmatians. It is from this time of conflict that the female-warrior graves of the Ukraine have been said to date. In these Sarmatian wars of conquest, we must conclude that Amazon warlords played an important role.

From the remains of their graves, we have a clear picture of the arms and armour used by the Sarmatian Amazons. Their most characteristic body armour was a tunic of thick hide, to which rows of overlapping iron scales were sewn. Over this was worn a thick leather belt, to which iron plates may also have been attached. This scale armour continued to be worn into the Christian era and is depicted on Trajan's Column. There, the armoured Sarmatian cavalry are seen to wear scaled trousers and horse armour. This form of body armour seems to have been preferred by the Sarmatians, even though mail was available to them via both Roman and Celtic military cultures and may have been worn on the legs and arms. Oval shields, covered with iron plates, were carried by the Scythians but do not appear to have been employed by Sarmatian armoured cavalry.

The bow available to the Sarmatians was a composite weapon made of wood, sinew and horn that was highly effective, particularly when shot from horseback. Iron and bronze arrowheads are the most common objects found in both male and female graves. The Sarmatians were noted also for their skill in close combat, using heavy bladed lances and long iron swords. Some sword blades have been found which are over four feet long. Strabo says they wielded their longest swords in both hands. Narrow, pointed axe blades have been discovered in graves, along with daggers. The most highly decorated weapons, with carved wooden and bone handles, come from the eastern regions of Kazakhstan, where Siberian animal decoration was prevalent, including representations of mountain goats, camels, stags and horses. In the west, Sarmatian decoration was influenced by Scythian,

25

Scythian-Sarmatian felt saddle cloth with embroidered motif of griffin attacking a mountain goat. From Pazirik, fifth century BC.

Persian, Greek and Celtic motifs, and many Amazon warriors may have worn armour adapted from these cultures. The Sarmatian horse harness included an iron bit and decorated metal plaques, but no stirrups.

Despite the wealth of archaeological evidence for this period, there are surprisingly few literary references to the Amazons. Throughout the fourth and third centuries BC, the Sarmatians must have been in bitter conflict with the Scythians as they took over their land, but there is no surviving record of it. Our major view of the Amazons at this time occurs in the several accounts of Alexander the Great and his conquest of the Persian Empire. Diodorus, Plutarch and Pompeius Trogus all refer to an occasion in 330 BC when Alexander was pausing in Parthia, just south of the Caspian Sea. He was recovering from a bout of diarrhoea following an expedition against a nomadic people. While resting, he was visited by several envoys, among them representatives of the Scythian king. Alexander was offered the hand of a Scythian princess, but the Macedonian warlord politely refused. Next, to his camp, came Thalestris, Queen of the Amazons. She arrived with 300 women warriors in full armour. Alexander was impressed by the splendour of the escort and asked Thalestris what she wanted. She replied that she wanted a child by him. She said that Alexander had demonstrated through his conquest of the world that he was the greatest of all men, and as she was superior to all women in strength and courage, their offspring would surpass all other mortals. Alexander was enthused by the idea and spent 13 days with her, after which he honoured her with presents and she left.

Both Diodorus and Pompeius Trogus wrote their versions of this coupling around 200 years after the event and based their research on earlier manuscripts. Plutarch, writing in the first century AD, is far more sceptical. He does not doubt that the Amazons existed, but he does question the authority of the meeting. He quotes several historians, both for and against it, and finally concludes it did not happen. In a letter written by Alexander, Plutarch says the Macedonian mentioned the Scythian offer of a princess, but says nothing of the Amazons. He then tells the story of Lysimachus, a companion of Alexander. Years after the campaigning, Lysimachus was listening to a reading of a history of Alexander, and when the historian reached the tale of Thalestris, he smiled and asked: 'And where was I at the time?'

By the second century AD, Arrian, in his great biography of Alexander, ignored the meeting completely, although he did record other references to the Amazons. While staying at Zariaspa, Alexander was approached both by a Scythian envoy and Pharasmanes, King of the Chorasinians. The king's realm bordered that of Colchis and the Amazons and he asked Alexander to invade these territories, subduing all the people around the Black Sea. He offered to act as a guide and provide Alexander with supplies and soldiers. Alexander thanked Pharasmanes and made an alliance with him, but said he could not undertake any expedition to the Black Sea. He had his mind on India.

Later, Arrian tells us that Alexander travelled to the plains of Nysa, around the southern coast of the Caspian Sea. There, he saw the breeding pastures of the famous Nysaean horses, the most sought after cavalry steeds in Asia. While staying there, the satrap of Media, Atropates, presented him with a company of armed women, saying they were Amazons. According to Arrian, the women were equipped like horse-warriors, except they carried axes rather than spears and small bucklers rather than shields. He also mentions claims that the women had smaller right breasts. Alexander, apparently, sent the Amazons away from his army, in case they should meet any 'roughness' from his troops, but told them to tell their queen that he was coming to see her in the hope of offspring. Arrian, however, doubts the existence of the Amazons and suggests that Atropates simply dressed some women in the Amazon fashion.

The common theme throughout these stories is the location of the meeting, somewhere just south of the Caspian Sea. It is the most likely place for Amazons to contact Alexander and for this reason, in the light of archaeological evidence, the possibility of it happening seems highly believable. Sarmatian Amazon graves have been discovered as far south as Georgia in the Caucasus. To the ancient authors, however, this meeting with Alexander the Great was the last recorded appearance of an Amazon queen. Pompeius Trogus writes that Thalestris died soon after returning to her kingdom, and with her disappeared the name of the Amazons. Diodorus maintains that the Amazons never really recovered from their battle against the Greeks led by Heracles and Theseus. Penthesileia was the last of the Amazons to win distinction for bravery, fighting alongside the Trojans against Achilles. 'After that the race diminished more and more and then lost all its strength,' Diodorus writes, 'so that in later times, whenever any writers recount their prowess, men consider the ancient stories about the Amazons to be fictitious tales.'

If Amazon leaders fail to be mentioned after the fourth century BC, there are still instances of women warriors encountered around the Black Sea. Appian, writing in the second century AD, describes a most interesting campaign led by the Roman general Pompey. In 66 BC, during the Mithridatic Wars, Pompey undertook an expedition of exploration along the eastern coast of the Black Sea, through the Caucasus Mountains. He wanted to trace the journey of the Argonauts and see the land of the Golden Fleece. Appian was sufficiently realistic about the probable origins of the ancient myths to suggest that Caucasian miners frequently panned for gold in the mountain rivers with a sheep's fleece and the resulting glittering wool was the source of Jason's quest. He was, therefore, not easily convinced by fabulous tales. Nevertheless, he records that Pompey was ambushed by Caucasian natives at the River Cyrtus, which runs into the Caspian Sea. The natives were skilled forest fighters, but Pompey overcame them by surrounding their hide-outs with his troops and then burning the trees. Among his many prisoners, he found women who had suffered wounds no less than the men. They were believed to be Amazons. This incident is described by Plutarch as well. It certainly is the right area for the continued existence of Sarmatian tribes.

Much later than this, in the sixth century AD, Procopius writes that the Amazons originated among the Caucasus Mountains, in the territory of the Alans and Sabric Huns. Even though no memory or place name of the Amazons survived in this area in his own time, Procopius derides those historians who dismiss the Amazons as complete myth. He follows Pompeius Trogus in believing that a barbarian race founded a city at Thermodon and because all their men were killed in battle, the women took arms to protect themselves. He bases this belief on the fact that after battles between Romans and Huns, the Romans found the bodies of women warriors among the dead Huns. Archaeologically speaking, the Alans certainly, and some western Huns maybe, were descended from the

Roman, bronze parade helmet in the form of a female face. Parade masks were worn during cavalry exercises and these female masks may have been worn by horsemen representing Amazons in some myth-based confrontation. Found on the face of a skeleton at Nola in southern Italy, second century AD.

Sarmatians and so their practices could well have survived among them.

Combining all the evidence available, it seems incontrovertible that the Amazons truly existed on the steppes north-east of the Black Sea. They can be identified with the Sarmatians and followed their cultural and military developments. That some of these warrior women forsook a life of marriage to pursue martial political careers is probable from the several accounts of Amazon queens. Rather than viewing their society as completely matri-archal, it seems more likely that it was a culture in which men and women shared power according to individual merit and tribal status. It is not known for how long the Amazon warlords ruled the steppes of Asia prior to their appearance in Greek history of the second millennium BC, but it is certain they existed in power until the third century BC. Thereafter, their presence appears to have declined, surviving only in a few isolated examples of warrior women. To what did they owe their decline? It may be that when the Sarmatians finally overtook the lands of the Scythians in the first century BC, the steppe warriors did not replace the Scythian culture with their own society. Instead, like so many barbarians after them, they were so impressed by the civilisation along the northern coast of the Black Sea that they adopted it themselves, regarding their ancient tradition of warrior women as a sign of backward barbarism and banished it forever.

Amazons
of the Jungle

**BRAZIL AND
DAHOMEY**

Rumours ran wild in Quito. Bored *conquistadores* latched on to any tale promising wealth beyond the Andes Mountains. It was said that a golden city existed somewhere east in the vast unexplored jungle. Each day, its king was annointed with oil and his body covered with gold dust. At night, the king washed in a sacred pool where the gold settled in rich layers, year after year. Through his domain ran a river so wide you could not see the other side. On its banks stood forests of rare spice trees. By 1541, the *conquistadores* were impatient to explore the new land. A few years earlier, Francisco Pizarro had conquered the Inca Empire in Peru. He placed his brother, Gonzalo, in charge of the Ecuadorian settlement of Quito and it was Gonzalo who led the expedition eastwards.

Among the Spanish *conquistadores* were several soldiers who had fought with Francisco against the Incas. They had been rewarded with grants of land, but they were still thirsty for more. One of these men was Francisco de Orellana. He had lost an eye during the conquest of the Incas, but he sold his estates and equipped a small force for the new adventure. As he journeyed across the mountains to join Pizarro, Orellana first heard the tale of the women who lived alone. According to the natives, they ruled a tribe of warrior women who raided other villages in search of mates. Orellana became convinced that somewhere in the rain forest beyond the mountains lay the kingdom of the Amazons. That was El Dorado.

The army Gonzalo Pizarro led into the Amazonian jungle was great by *conquistador* standards. At its core were 150 Spanish horsemen with 190 foot-soldiers. All of them were veterans of the Inca war. They wore battered, steel morion helmets with breastplates and carried both arquebus firearms and crossbows. Four thousand Indians were recruited to serve them. They carried the baggage as well as providing an armed force with bows, arrows, spears and armour of animal skins. Two thousand vicious hunting dogs were included as the Indians possessed a deep fear of them. Pigs for food and llamas as beasts of burden completed the legion. It was a formidable force, but began to suffer almost immediately from the ferocity

31

of the wilderness. In the mountains, many Indians died from the cold and rarified atmosphere. In the jungle, the llamas succumbed to the stifling heat. The pigs escaped and the *conquistadores* became desperate. Natives were captured and torn apart by their dogs. Pizarro insisted on finding El Dorado.

With just 23 Spanish soldiers and a crowd of Indians, Francisco de Orellana trailed after Pizarro's expedition. He had arrived too late at Quito to join them and now followed the jungle path hacked by Pizarro's army. Relentless rain and earth-shaking storms slowed down their progress, rotting the clothes on their bodies. By the time they reached Pizarro's camp at Zumaco, somewhere along the River Napo, they had nothing left except their swords and shields. Pizarro was furious, hoping Orellana would have brought some supplies. They were in a worse condition than his own men.

Still believing in forests of cinnamon, Pizarro took a small force and plunged into the forest. He left Orellana in the camp, instructing him to construct a ship and to search for food. Trees were felled and nails made from the shoes of horses slaughtered for meat. A brigantine arose on the bank of the river, to be powered by oars rather than sails. The gaps in its planks were filled with oakum, made from old shirts and blankets, and sealed with tar improvised from the resin of trees. With the ship afloat, Orellana was ordered to sail down the river until he had collected sufficient provisions. Then he was to wait for Pizarro and his army where, according to the natives, two rivers met. Accompanied by 57 Spaniards, Orellana said farewell to Pizarro. The two *conquistadores* were never to see each other again.

For six days, the ship drifted with the current of the river. Despite the lush greenery pouring into the river on either side, there was no food to be had. At a point where two rivers met, Orellana paused. There was no sign of Pizarro. It was possible that Pizarro had made a mistake and was lost in the jungle. Orellana's men agreed to continue along the river in search of food. Eventually, the sound of drums drew their attention and they landed near an Indian village. The natives were friendly and offered them food. Orellana claimed the village for Spain and asked his men again if they should return to search for Pizarro. They all voted to continue, appointing Orellana their leader. Orellana was careful to note this down and have every Spaniard sign it. While he oversaw the building of a second ship, Orellana heard more information about the Amazons living in the jungle. One of the Indian chieftains asked him if he intended to visit the Amurianos, who in his language were called Coniupuyara, meaning 'great women'. He advised Orellana to be careful because the Spaniards would be outnumbered by the women and killed.

In the meantime, Pizarro arrived at the point where he believed Orellana would be waiting for him. He had kept his ragged army going with the promise of food, slaughtering their last few dogs and horses before reaching the river. At the water's side, the *conquistadores* fell on their knees in

Spanish *conquistador* riding a llama in Peru. From a woodcut of 1599.

despair. There was nothing waiting for them. Only the brown waves of the river and the mocking cries of animals invisible around them. There was nothing else Pizarro could do but to turn round and travel all the way back to Quito. His 16 months in the jungle had been for nothing. There was no forest of cinnamon, no El Dorado. Orellana was damned forever as a deserter.

With a second, bigger ship, Orellana and his men continued along the river. With each day, the waterway grew wider, more impressive. Without knowing it, the *conquistadores* had passed from the River Napo into the upper stretch of the River Amazon itself. Beyond each new bend, they hung on to the hope that the golden towers of El Dorado would rise above the forest. They were attacked by Indians in canoes, blowing trumpets, hurling spears, and carrying large shields of alligator and tapir skin. The powder for the Spanish guns was damp and they had to rely solely on their crossbows.

They fought a running battle along the river and only after much brave fighting on both sides did the *conquistadores* finally triumph.

Wounded and hungry, the ships drifted on. Indian witch-doctors surrounded them in canoes, blowing clouds of smoke through long pipes to stop them. But the Spaniards' gunpowder had now dried and they turned the Indians away with their own magic. They passed the mouth of a second great tributary, the Japura. The shore was growing more populated and with each new village, the *conquistadores* had to fight off the native canoes. They stopped occasionally to raid the settlements for food, but each landing involved a fierce battle. A third great river was sighted to the left of the ships. This time, its waters were pitch black and its current so strong that its inky waters did not mix with the brown of the Amazon for 20 leagues. The Spaniards called it the River Negro.

The village buildings along the river were becoming more sophisticated and in one, the *conquistadores* saw a model city set upon a platform in the middle of a clearing. Orellana asked the Indians what it represented.

'It is the city of our rulers,' they replied.

'And who are they?'

'The women who live alone.'

The Indians explained that the Amazons ruled over all the land and there were many villages with such monuments dedicated to their female leader. When the Amazons visited their village, the natives gave them the feathers of parrots and macaws to decorate the roofs of their altars.

By June 1542, Orellana had passed the River Madiera, somewhere between the Ilha das Oncas and the city of the Parintins, latitudes 57° and 56°W, longitude 2.5°N, over half-way along the River Amazon. It was decided by one of the two priests on board, Fray Gaspar de Carvajal, to celebrate the feast-day of St John the Baptist on shore. The river was broad and Orellana sailed close to a particularly large settlement. The Indians tumbled out of their huts and pushed their canoes into the water. Orellana tried to communicate his peaceful intentions, but the Indians merely laughed at him, raising their weapons. Continuing his course towards the shore, Orellana ordered his men to aim their guns and crossbows. Some of the natives fell before the bolts and bullets and their comrades rowed back to the shore, calling for assistance. Orellana was determined to land to replenish his stores. Several *conquistadores* stepped into rowing-boats and approached the shore, firing all the time. The Spaniards found it difficult to row and protect themselves against the Indian arrows, and several were wounded. Fray Gaspar was one of this landing party and received an arrow in his torso. Only the thick material of his habit protected him from a serious wound. The priest recorded what happened next.

'At this point,' he recalled, 'it is necessary to explain that these natives defended themselves with such bravery because they were the vassals of the Amazons. Having been informed of our arrival, they called on these Amazons for assistance. We saw ten or twelve of them fighting in the front

Conquistadores beating Indian baggage carriers. From a series of anti-Spanish engravings by Theodore de Bry about 1600. Gonzalo Pizarro recruited an army of 4,000 Indians to carry supplies on his expedition to the Amazon.

ranks as though they were commanders. The Indians did not dare turn their backs on us, as those that fled were killed with wooden clubs by the Amazons. These women appeared very white and tall, with long hair twisted over their heads. They are very robust and go without clothing except for a bandage around their loins. In their hands, they carry bows and arrows and their shower of arrows made our vessels look like porcupines.

'It pleased the Lord to give our men the strength to kill seven or eight of these Amazons. As a result, the attack of the savages weakened and our soldiers dispersed them. But as reinforcements were arriving from neighbouring villages and their ranks were forming again under the command of their chieftains, Orellana told us to board the ship rapidly to avoid casualties.'

As Orellana steered his ships towards the middle of the river, he questioned an Indian prisoner about the Amazon attackers. The Indian admitted he knew about the women because he took them tribute on his chieftain's behalf. His chieftain was called Couynco and his land was a vassal state of the Amazons, who lived some seven days' journey inland. The women were not married. Orellana wanted to know more. At last, they were nearing El Dorado. Through a language of general Indian words and signs, the prisoner explained all he knew of the land of the Amazons.

'The women were very numerous and dwelled in seventy villages,' recorded Fray Gaspar. 'Their houses were built of stone and provided with doors. The roads from one village to another were fenced on both sides and guarded at regular intervals so no one could approach without paying toll.'

'But who are the fathers of these women's children?' asked Orellana.

'The women make war against a great lord nearby,' replied the Indian, 'and bring back warriors as captives and live with them in their villages. When a woman becomes pregnant, the prisoners are sent back to their land. When a son is born, he is killed and his body sent to the father. When a daughter is born, she is cared for and taught the ways of war.'

'Who is the lord of these women?'

'They are subject to a female chieftain called Conori,' said the Indian. 'The Amazons possess great wealth in silver and gold. The household utensils of the most important Amazon women are made of precious metals. They have five great houses or temples dedicated to the sun, containing idols of gold and silver representing the figures of women. Their clothing is made of fine llama wool and it covers their bodies from breast to knee and is sometimes fixed by buttons, sometimes by laces. They have long hair and wear gold crowns two inches in width adorned with coloured designs. They ride camels and other creatures with long hair and double-toed feet.'

All these details Fray Gaspar recorded. It was the high point of Orellana's expedition and the reason why the mighty river is so named. After this confrontation, Orellana's ships sailed past hostile tribes until they reached the Atlantic Ocean, 243 days after setting out on the river. Immediately, Orellana caught a ship home to present his discovery to the King of Spain. The king was delighted and made Orellana governor of the great river and all its territory. But despite the stories Orellana told of the Amazons and their mighty empire somewhere in the jungle, money was not forthcoming for his return voyage. There was also the problem of letters from Gonzalo Pizarro to the king, claiming that Orellana was a deserter.

Gonzalo was dead, the victim of a mutiny in Peru, but his accusations clung to the Spanish adventurer. Eventually, the courts decided in Orellana's favour and by bankrupting his family, he got the money to equip a fleet to return to the Amazon. The expedition was doomed from the beginning. The majority of his men died from illness and he lost half his ships. In the company of his new wife, he reached the mouth of the Amazon, but the Indians were as hostile as ever and he lost more men to

Conquistadores setting savage dogs on Indians. Pizarro included 2,000 such dogs in his army.

their arrows. The strain was becoming too much. His spirit was determined to lay the foundation of his capital on the land of the Amazons, but in December 1545, surrounded by the alien jungle, his body gave out. His wife wrapped his corpse in the Spanish flag and committed it to the brown water of the river he had discovered.

Orellana's tales of an Amazon empire in the Brazilian jungle continued to excite explorers long after his death. But how true were they? There is good reason to surmise that Orellana had need of such a fantastic discovery to justify his expedition along the river. Intentionally or not, he had deserted Gonzalo Pizarro, brother of the most powerful man in Spanish South America. Above all, if Orellana were to make any profit from his journey along the river, he had to excite the interest of potential investors in his new land. This could only be done with the lure of an El Dorado, and Orellana chose to portray it as an empire of the Amazons. The surviving crew of

Orellana's first expedition, including Fray Gaspar, all attested to their sighting of the Amazons. But the fact remains that they were the first and last to see the Amazon warriors. Garcilaso Inca de la Vega, in his late-sixteenth century history of the Gonzalo expedition, puts his version of the truth bluntly: 'Francisco de Orellana, in descending the river, had some skirmishes with the Indians inhabiting that shore, who were very fierce, and in some parts the women came out to fight with their husbands. On this account, and to make his voyage the more wonderful, he said that it was a land of Amazons and besought His Majesty for a commission to conquer them.'

Almost a hundred years later, a Spanish priest, Cristobal d'Acuna, sailed along the Amazon and reached the very point where Orellana claimed he was attacked by the Amazons. He mentions a tribe, the Guacaras, who communicate and trade with the women. 'The Amazons are women of great valour,' he writes. 'They have preserved themselves without the ordinary intercourse with men. And even when they receive them, once every year, they brandish their bows and arrows at them until they are satisfied that the men come with peaceful intentions. They then drop their weapons and take them to the hammocks in their houses and receive the Indians as guests for a few days. After this, the men return to their own country.' D'Acuna goes on to repeat Fray Gaspar's description of the fate of their children. 'Time will discover the truth of this,' he concludes, 'but if these are the Amazons made famous by historians, then there are treasures shut in their territory which would enrich the whole world.' Despite such conviction, however, d'Acuna's account was based on hearsay. He did not actually see the Amazons.

In 1595, Sir Walter Raleigh visited Guiana and was fascinated by reports of women warriors. He spoke to a tribal headman who told him that 'the nation of these women is on the south side of the Amazon in the province of Tapajos. Their chief places of strength and retreat being on the islands situated to the south some sixty leagues up from the mouth of the river.' With ample references to the classical myths of the Amazons, Raleigh repeats earlier accounts of their relations with men once a year. He says they are reported to be very fierce and bloodthirsty, but again, he is reporting hearsay and did not actually see any warrior women. Antonio de Herrera, in his history of Orellana, says 'some Spaniards were of the opinion that Captain Orellana should not have given the name of the Amazons to the women he fought, because in the Indies it was no new thing for the women to fight, and to use bows and arrows, as has been seen on some islands of Barlovento and at Carthagena, where they displayed as much courage as the men.'

Herrera's comment gets us nearer to the truth than any other. It is more than likely that an Indian tribe, under attack from an alien force armed with firearms and crossbows, should unite all its people, men and women, to defend itself. What is highly unlikely, and must derive from Orellana's

38

imagination, is the presence of a kingdom of warrior women dominating the surrounding tribes in a manner similar to the mythical Amazons of Thermodon. As revealed by archaeology in the Ukraine, there are true occasions of women warriors fighting alongside men within primitive nomadic societies, but there is no evidence in the Brazilian rain forest, or anywhere else in the world, of a genuinely matriarchal society in which women exclusively dominated men. Throughout recorded history, women rulers have only risen to positions of power when there was no legitimate male heir. There has never been an historically proven instance of a society in which the sex roles have been completely reversed. Indeed, many feminist historians maintain that ancient examples of matriarchies have only been mentioned by male historians to prove their ultimate impracticality and eventual failure.

Among the Indians of Brazil, anthropologists have discovered myths of female domination invented for the very purpose of justifying male rule. Among tribes of central Brazil, the Mundurucu myth tells of an occasion when the native women took possession of the sacred tribal trumpets. Because of this, they could force the men to collect firewood, fetch water and make bread. But the men still hunted and needed to feed meat to the trumpets. So they took the trumpets from the women and returned them to their subservient role. Other South American tales tell of the incompetence of female rule and how the chaos had to be settled by men who forced the women into submission. Such a mythical base for male domination is not too dissimilar from the more outlandish Greek accounts of Amazon life beyond the Black Sea.

It is likely that Francisco de Orellana may have heard such tales of female domination from the Indians and believed them to refer to current events. The Indians of the rain forest are notorious for telling visitors exactly what they want to hear, rather than what is true, particularly when the visitors threaten them with weapons. For this reason, the Indians probably embroidered their old tribal myths with descriptions of gold and silver. Occasional incidents of tribal women taking up arms to assist their men would then have confirmed this image in the mind of a man desperate for fantastic discoveries.

The presence of Amazon warriors within the jungles of South America remained a common traveller's tale ever after Orellana's sighting. By the eighteenth century, this legend was matched across the Atlantic by equally fantastic accounts of warrior women in the forests of West Africa. Captain William Snelgrave was the first European to report their existence. In 1727, his ship anchored along the Gold Coast at Jaqueen, probably now in Benin. He was in the business of shipping slaves to the West Indies and was keen to further trade relations with the African kings of the interior. Receiving an invitation from the King of Dahomey, one of the most powerful native kingdoms in the region, he set out into the equatorial forest, carried in a hammock by six black servants. The capital of the kingdom of Dahomey lay some 40 miles (65 km) northwards from the coast. Before approaching the settlement, Snelgrave and the Europeans with him changed into their finest clothes. The king's chief courtier received the white men with respect and they retired to a hut for a lunch of cold ham and fowls. Snelgrave complained of the flies, great numbers of them settling on his food while he ate. The reason for their presence was soon revealed. As they approached the King's Gate for their first interview with the Dahomeyan monarch, they

Brazilian Indians in battle array. The shields are made of slender sticks bound together with creeper strings.

40

saw two stages piled high with human heads: the rotting trophies of 4,000 enemy tribesmen sacrificed to the god of the Dahomey. It was a shocking sight, the first of many outraged accounts of human-sacrifice in West Africa. Understandably nervous, the Europeans were then introduced to the monarch, instigator of so much ritual slaughter. Captain Snelgrave recorded the scene. Sitting on a gilt throne, the king was surrounded by women. Three held large umbrellas over his head. A further four stood behind him, carrying flintlock muskets on their shoulders. They were naked from the waist upwards, wearing gold rings around their arms and beads around their neck and in their hair. They were members of the king's elite bodyguard, composed completely of women.

When Captain Snelgrave returned to the Gold Coast in 1730, he heard further accounts of women warriors. According to Europeans living along the coast, the King of Dahomey had been hard pressed in his wars with neighbouring tribes. The wars were fought to obtain slaves to sell to the Europeans and the King of Dahomey had lost many good men in a recent expedition. In order to protect himself against the advancing enemy tribes, the king expanded his personal bodyguard of women. 'He ordered a great Number of Women to be armed like Soldiers,' wrote Snelgrave, 'and appointed Officers to each Company, with Colours, Drums and Umbrellas, according to the Negroe Fashion. Then ordering the Army to march, the Women Soldiers were placed in the Rear, to prevent Discovery.' Apparently, the ruse worked and the enemy were surprised at the large Dahomeyan army, fleeing before it. This is the first European account of Dahomey's Amazons in battle and might well have been discounted by cynical readers as pure fantasy. But Snelgrave's account was the first of several to come from the Gold Coast, culminating in a series of detailed reports in the nineteenth century. Unlike Orellana, Snelgrave had discovered a true army of Amazons in the jungle of West Africa.

By 1850, Britain had ceased to be part of the slave trade. British travellers to the Gold Coast keenly wrote of the continuing horrors among its native tribes and their barbarous customs of human-sacrifice. Such reports encouraged imperial action against both slavers and the African kingdoms. One such anti-slaver was Frederick Forbes. In order to gain a clearer picture of the slave-hunting wars led by the African kings, he led two missions to the court of Dahomey. Naturally enough, Forbes was fascinated by their more outrageous customs and described the King of Dahomey's special bodyguard.

'The amazons', he wrote, 'are not supposed to marry, and, by their own statement, they have changed their sex. "We are men," say they, "not women". All dress alike, diet alike, and male and female emulate each other: what the males do, the amazons will endeavour to surpass. They all take great care of their arms, polish the barrels, and except when on duty, keep them in covers. There is no duty at the palace, except when the king is in public, and then a guard of amazons protect the royal person, and, on

review, he is guarded by the males; but outside the palace is always a strong detachment of males ready for service. The amazons are in barracks within the palace enclosure, and under the care of the eunuchs and the camboodee or treasurer. In every action (with males and females), there is some reference to cutting off heads. In their dances—and it is the duty of the soldier and the amazon to be a proficient dancer—with eyes dilated, the right hand is working in a sawlike manner for some time, as if in the act of cutting round the neck, when both hands are used, and a twist is supposed to finish the bloody deed.'

On his second visit to Dahomey in 1850, Forbes witnessed a parade of the Amazon guard before their king. Beneath a canopy of umbrellas on the south side of the market-place of Abomey, the Dahomey capital, sat the monarch on a skull-ornamented war-stool. Around him stood ministers, dwarfs and hunchbacks. To his right sat the 'Light of the Harem' and her female courtiers. Before him assembled his Amazon regiments. As a mark of distinction, each Amazon had three stripes of whitewash daubed around her legs. As soon as they arrived in front of the throne, they saluted the king and one of their officers stepped forward to swear their allegiance.

'Have we not conquered all the province of Mahee?' swore the officer. 'So we will always conquer or die.'

A second officer stepped forward.

'When the Attahpahms heard we were advancing, they ran away. If we go to war, and any return not conquerors, let them die. If I retreat, my life is at the king's mercy. Whatever the town to be attacked, we will conquer, or bury ourselves in its ruins.'

A third officer announced that her warriors had never been known to turn their backs on the enemy and if anyone could contradict this then they should say so. A male officer next to the king was about to respond to this, when a witchdoctor warned him: 'That woman is fetish, you are not. You must not interfere with her.'

Further regiments grouped before the king. They were named after their female commanders and bore the titles of fire-horn and turkey-buzzard. They presented their weapons for inspection, large knives and muskets. Each officer endeavoured to express a more articulate vow of fidelity than the previous one.

'War is our great friend,' said one. 'Without it there is no cloth, no armlets. Let us to war, conquer or die.'

'I long to kill an elephant to show my fidelity,' said another. 'But the Attahpahms must be extermined first. One of the male soldiers sent us Guinea pepper to excite us to war. Such is an insult.'

After their vows, the women warriors sang and danced before the king. Finally, the chief commander of all the Amazons stood before the monarch.

'A cask of rum cannot roll itself,' she said. 'A table only becomes useful when something is placed on it. The Dahomeyan army without the Amazons are as both. Spitting makes the belly more comfortable, and the outstretched hand will be the receiving one. So we ask you for war, that our bellies may have their desire and our hands be filled.'

Forbes concluded that a total of 2,400 women warriors paraded before the Dahomeyan king. If Forbes's version of the oaths of allegiance communicates only a vague record of their content, it undoubtedly suggests that the Amazon warriors were more than just a bizarre bodyguard but were also an integral part of the army, an élite force keen for battle.

Following the parade, Forbes was invited to view a sham fight between the Amazon warriors and prisoners from a previous campaign. On the south side of the market-place stood a stockade made of palm branches. This represented a town and contained many slaves. On the north side, the Amazons assembled under their different regimental colours. In accordance with the symbolic nature of the exercise, an advanced guard approached

Male Dahomeyan warrior. Many European observers considered the Dahomeyan Amazons more effective warriors than their male counterparts and King Gezo in the mid-nineteenth century raised them to equal status. Late nineteenth-century photograph.

the town in the act of reconnoitring. Then came the main army in two battalions, with muskets over their shoulders. At the rear, guarded by a reserve, came their fetish objects plus war-stools.

In the centre of the parade-ground, a tent was erected in which the Amazon officers held a council of war. Scouts were sent and returned with information. Aides-de-camp ran to and fro from council to army. Finally, the officers approached the king, reporting on the state of the country and position of the enemy. The king replied that as this was only a skirmish, the young Amazons were to take the lead. 'At noon,' records Forbes, 'a musket was fired, and a portion of the army attacked the stockade, made an entrée, and speedily reappeared, some with prisoners, some with tufts of grass to imitate heads.'

The assault was repeated and several slaves escaped from the enclosure. At the culmination of the exercise, the entire Amazon army assembled before the stockade. Only the reserve remained to guard the prisoners. At a signal, the Amazons advanced at speed and broke down the stockade. All the prisoners were then allowed to escape, being chased and hunted with great enthusiasm, finally being bound and dragged before the king. At the end of the exercise, the king presented Forbes with a sample of war rations: 'hard round cakes made of palm oil, peppers, corn, salt, and beans, very nutritious, but difficult to masticate.'

Four years earlier, John Duncan, formerly of the Life Guards, was also treated to a display of the fighting skills of the Dahomeyan Amazons. 'They

Mock battle staged by Dahomeyan Amazons and male warriors. Note that the Amazons are provided with muskets, whereas the males carry only swords, suggesting that the males embraced close combat while the females were trained as sharp-shooters.

The French river-boat *Opale*. Forced to retreat by Dahomeyan artillery, it was useful for carrying supplies for Colonel Dodds's campaign against the Dahomey in 1892. Drawing from 1896.

seem to use the long Danish musket with as much ease as one of our grenadiers does his firelock,' he concluded, 'but not, of course, with the same quickness, as they are not trained to any particular exercise, but, on receiving the word, make an attack like a pack of hounds, with great swiftness. Of course they would be useless against disciplined troops, if at all approaching to the same numbers. Still their appearance is more martial than the generality of the men; and if undertaking a campaign, I should prefer the females to the male soldiers of this country.'

Duncan's visit to Dahomey enabled him to record the appearance of the Amazon uniform: 'They wear a blue and white striped cotton surtout, the stripes about one and a half inch wide, of stout native manufacture, without sleeves, leaving freedom for the arms. The skirt or tunic reaches as low as the kilt of the Highlanders. A pair of short trousers is worn underneath, reaching two inches below the knee.' In 1871, J. A. Skertchly, an insect collector, was forced to stay with the King of Dahomey for eight months and used that period to elaborate on Duncan's description of the Amazon army. 'They are divided into three brigades,' he wrote, 'known as the king's company, the right, and the left wings. Each of these has a peculiar head-dress, by which they may be known. The king's brigade, sometimes called the Fanti company, or centre, wear the hair shaved *à la turban*, and bound with narrow fillets, with alligators of coloured cloth sewn on them. The

47

right wing have their heads shaven, leaving only a solitary tuft or two, while the left wing wear the hair *au naturelle.'*

According to Skertchly, the army numbered some 4,000, although the finest warriors of the corps had perished in a battle against a rival tribe in 1864. Skertchly identified four kinds of warriors within each division, those in the king's brigade being the élite. The Agbaraya, or blunder-buseers, were the veterans of the army and only called into action when urgently needed. They were the biggest and strongest warriors of the force and each was accompanied by an attendant carrying ammunition. They wore blue tunics and their standards were the most ferocious, bearing images of a figure cutting an enemy to pieces, or blowing him apart with a musket shot. The Gbeto, or elephant huntresses, were reputed to be the bravest warriors. They carried out dangerous hunting expeditions and many bore the ferocious scars of close encounters with wounded elephants. The Nyekplehhentoh, or razor women, were noted for their special hatred of the enemy's leader. They carried a hinged sword about 18 inches ($\frac{1}{2}$ m) long that shut into its scabbard like a razor. The blade was used for decapitation. The Gulonentoh, or musketeers, formed the majority of the warriors. In the 1860s, according to the explorer Richard Burton, they were armed with Tower muskets supplied with bad ammunition: using bamboo fibre for the wadding, for instance. In addition, the king's brigade had a fifth type of warrior, the Gohento, or archers. These were mainly young girls equipped with a bow, a quiver of poisoned, light cane arrows and a small knife strapped to their wrist. They were rarely employed in combat, but used as scouts and porters.

Under Gezo, King of Dahomey around 1850, the Amazons are said to have attained their greatest prestige. He raised them to a status equal, if not superior, to his male warriors. He issued a decree summoning every subject to present their daughters to him. From them he chose the most promising teenage girls to serve as officers, while others became ordinary soldiers. Every three years afterwards, a similar conscription was made. The majority of the Amazons were required to remain celebate. If they ever transgressed this code, then they and their seducers were executed. This resulted in the old Dahomeyan joke that more soldiers lost their lives climbing over the walls into the quarters of the Amazons than died in battle. A few Amazons, however, were reserved as concubines for the king and they were called Leopard wives.

Richard Burton was convinced that the enforced celebacy of the Amazons added to their ferocity. 'They are savage as wounded gorillas, more cruel far than their brethren in arms.' Skertchly even thought the British might adapt such a military system to their own needs. 'Now that the subject of female employment is so prominent before the public mind, it would, in many cases, be happy release from their relatives if all the old maids could be enlisted, and trained to vent their feline spite and mischief-making propensities on the enemies of the country, instead of their neighbours.'

French soldiers battle with Dahomeyan warriors in the final combat before the capture of the West African capital of Abomey. Illustration by Stanley L. Wood, 1895.

Stanley L Wood '95

Throughout the nineteenth century, the Amazons of Dahomey were mainly employed in the annual slave wars waged against their neighbours. The King of Dahomey paid his warriors for the slaves and sold them to Europeans on the coast. By the end of the century, however, this status quo was under attack. Since 1862, the French had expanded their interests along the Gold Coast. By 1890, relations between France and Dahomey had deteriorated. Behanzin, King of Dahomey, enforced his right to levy tribute on the French trading post at Porto Novo, now the capital of Benin. His army was defeated and a treaty concluded, but he was determined to gain revenge. He realised his army needed the latest European weaponry and set about buying breech-loading rifles and artillery. At last, in 1892 he believed he was ready for a second clash with the French. Rifles were issued to his male and female warriors. It was to be the greatest military test for the Dahomeyan Amazons.

In spring 1892, Behanzin invaded the territory of Porto Novo. The French retaliated by sending a small army under the command of Colonel Dodds, a French officer descended from an English trader. He had previously served in the upper Senegal and western Sudan and was used to African warfare. He led a force of 150 French marines and 800 Foreign Legionnaires, plus 1,500 Senegalese riflemen and 300 Houssas under French officers. A company of engineers, a battery of mountain artillery, some cavalry, a transport and ambulance detachment, and a river-boat armed with machine-guns completed the army, totalling just under 3,500 men. The Dahomeyan force opposing Dodds was estimated at 12,000 strong, consisting of 2,000 Amazons, 5,000 male warriors and 5,000 armed slaves. Behanzin had bought them modern rifles, machine-guns, and artillery from traders at Whydah, but this was not what concerned Colonel Dodds most. He feared the disease and dense forest that covered the land between Porto Novo and the capital, Abomey. To protect his men, quinine became part of the daily ration and brandy was only drunk diluted.

On 17 August, Colonel Dodds began his march into the interior. His orders provided not only for the defence of Porto Novo, but recommended the destruction of the Dahomeyan kingdom once and for all. This meant a trek of over 70 miles (110 km) from the coast to Abomey. Dodds decided to advance along the River Oueme so his gunboat *Opale* could protect his men as well as carrying supplies. Leaving a sizeable garrison in Porto Novo, he led 2,000 soldiers plus 2,000 native porters. The advance was laborious, across swamp and through rain-sodden bush. Behanzin shadowed the invaders, but preserved his best warriors—his Amazons—for the battle to come.

It took two months to reach the River Koto, some 12 miles (20 km) southeast of Abomey. There had been several skirmishes and the river-boat *Opale* had been forced to retreat because of the Dahomeyan artillery. French scouts pushed on through the densely knotted vegetation at the side of the river. In the distance, they could see the huts of the king's palace at Kotopa.

On the slope beyond the river, they also saw a triple line of entrenchments, with guns sited on higher ground behind them. Dodds decided to keep the attention of the Dahomeyan position while sending the majority of his army northwards about three thousand yards and then crossing the river so as to advance around the African defences. The battle began with the diversionary shots of two French mountain-guns. The Dahomey replied with accurate shooting, but their ammunition was of poor quality and did not explode. Nevertheless, the solid shot forced the French artillery to retreat.

In the meantime, the majority of Dodds's force was hacking its way through the bush along the river. Eventually, they arrived at a clearing and began the task of crossing the river. Dahomeyan scouts were fully aware of the Frenchmen's strategy and a contingent of Amazons rapidly advanced to meet the threat. The Amazons were armed with the finest breech-loading rifles and began to pick off the Frenchmen as they descended into the tangled foliage beside the river. Many of the Amazons were expert hunters and to their deadly accuracy they added the frightening power of exploding bullets, usually reserved for shooting elephants. The French were forced back up the side of the river valley. It was the most serious situation Dodds had faced. The water supply of his men was running short and he could not force his way across the river. Emboldened by their success, Amazon warriors advanced from the bush, using giant ant-hills as cover. At one time, they tried to rush the French position, but were met with a fiercesome volley. Reluctantly, Dodds admitted defeat and sent his men back to camp.

For a week, the two adversaries glared at each other across the River Koto. While Dodds awaited reinforcements, the Dahomey attacked the camp. They were repulsed with heavy losses. Dodds decided to turn the other wing of the Dahomeyan position and moved south-west. As he began to lose his whereabouts in the dense jungle, Dodds received news of a truce from Behanzin. Perhaps because he was suffering greater losses than the French imagined, the Dahomeyan king had evacuated his position at Kotopa in order to bring about peace. Dodds returned to camp and the next day sent his men across the main bridge on the Koto. As the head of the column passed on to the bridge, a mighty fusilade of rifles and artillery raked the French army. Furious at the Dahomeyan treachery, the French fixed bayonets and rushed on them. In ferocious hand-to-hand fighting, the French battled with Amazons and male warriors from trench to trench. In just half an hour, the resolve of the Dahomeyan warriors was broken and the French captured the lines at Kotopa. It was the turning-point of the campaign.

From then on, the fighting was bitter and relentless, but the French had command of the bush and took their time closing upon Abomey. In a final conflict at Yukue, the main Dahomeyan attack was launched by hundreds of prisoners and slaves who had been promised their freedom as a reward of victory. Half-drunk with gin and rum, they desperately threw themselves at the French square. The repeating rifles killed them effortlessly. On 15

November, having just been promoted to the rank of general, Dodds advanced the final miles towards Abomey. As his vanguard marched through the cultivated land on the outskirts of the city, a series of explosions rent the air. A dense cloud of smoke rose from the buildings of the capital. Behanzin, fleeing to the north, had destroyed his city rather than let it fall into the hands of the French.

Within a few weeks, Behanzin was captured. With his downfall, the ancient kingdom of Dahomey ceased to exist and with it the extraordinary tradition of the Amazon warriors. The land and its people were now part of the French Empire. The story of the Dahomeyan Amazons is remarkable as it is the only major example of women warriors substantiated by reliable literary and visual evidence. It demonstrates the real possibility of a female army in other societies and lends credence to ancient accounts of women warriors in Asia and Africa. It is, however, a far cry from the Amazon societies described by Greek authors and the Spaniard Orellana. Despite their élite military nature, the Dahomeyan Amazons were little more than a bizarre extension of the king's harem. Dahomeyan society was very definitely male-dominated. As the Amazons of Orellana's journey were probably little more than myth, it leaves only the Sarmatian Amazons as the one known true occurrence of a society in which men and women shared the business of war, with the high probability of several women reaching senior posts of command within the tribe. But there are, of course, many occasions in which women have risen to powerful military commands within traditionally male-dominated societies. These were not Amazons, but women who, through skilful politics or the accident of inheritance, found themselves in positions of power usually exercised by men. To defend their power, they had to become efficient warlords.

'Braver than her Husband'

When Xerxes, King of Persia, led his great army against the Greeks in 480 BC, he ignored the advice of one of his most trusted military advisers, Artemisia, Queen of Halicarnassus. Named after Artemis, the Cretan goddess of hunting, Artemisia was the daughter of Lygdamis, a wealthy Greek Halicarnassan, and a Cretan mother. Her husband had recently died and she assumed the rule of her city-state, now the Turkish port of Bodrum, until her young son was old enough to govern. Despite her Greek lineage and cultural background, Artemisia's Aegean kingdom lay within the orbit of the Persian Empire. When Xerxes called upon all his subjects, from Asia Minor across the Middle East to India, to raise an army for his invasion of Greece, Artemisia was compelled to recruit her own small force and join the army. To do otherwise would have invited the wrath of the Persian king, but, throughout the endeavour, she was unsure of the wisdom of the expedition.

Xerxes' army was one of the greatest the ancient world had ever seen. Herodotus, writing only a few years after the campaign, records it being 1,700,000 men strong. A vast number and certainly a wild overestimate, but clearly an indication of a huge gathering of troops. As the land army marched around the northern Aegean, across the Hellespont, it was accompanied by the Persian navy, equally vast in scale. Herodotus writes of 1,207 triremes supplied by Phoenicians, Syrians, Cyprians, Egyptians, and Greeks from Asia Minor. These were supported by 3,000 smaller ships of 30 and 50 oars, light galleys and transport boats. The Carian contingent of 70 ships included Artemisia's. She led five ships from Halicarnassus and the islands of Kos, Nisiros and Kalimnos. On board, her warriors were armed very much like her Greek adversaries, wearing bronze helmets, breastplates and greaves, but carrying scimitars and daggers different to the Greeks. Despite their small number, Herodotus claims the ships of Halicarnassus were among the best in the fleet, second only to those of Sidon.

At first, Artemisia's misgivings about the campaign were unfounded. Xerxes' army broke through stiff resistance at Thermopylae and seized Athens. The whole of Attica lay open to his plundering; the Acropolis was set on fire and the Athenians humiliated. While several Greek warlords switched their allegiance to the King of Persia, Xerxes wondered whether he should finish the Greeks once and for all by destroying their fleet anchored at Salamis, an island immediately to the south of the Athenian port of Piraeus. At Phaleron, a few miles along the coast from Piraeus, Xerxes reviewed his fleet. His chief military commander, Mardonius, asked the various naval commanders for their opinions on a sea battle. All, aside from Artemisia, were in favour of the combat.

'Tell the king,' she said to Mardonius, 'that it is I who say this and clearly I have not been lacking in courage against the Greeks.' Apparently, she had distinguished herself in a naval engagement off Artemisium, on the island of Euboea. 'But,' she continued, 'I council you not to offer their fleet a battle. The Greeks are much stronger at sea than us, just as men are stronger than women. So why endanger yourself at sea? You have possession of Athens, the aim of this campaign. On land, no man stands against you. You could even advance into the Peloponnese and easily gain victory. The Greeks cannot hold a united front and will scatter to their individual cities. I hear the Greeks on Salamis are short of food and if you lead your army into the Peloponnese, then those Greeks will be fully occupied and have no wish to support the Athenians in a sea battle. But to push for a naval confrontation now risks great harm to both your fleet and your land army.'

At the end of her speech, Artemisia cast doubt on the loyalty of several of Xerxes' allies, including the Egyptian, Cyprian, Cilician and Pamphylian contingents of the fleet. Her words caused uproar. The captains of these nations were already aggrieved at her exaggerated importance among the military council and hoped her outspokeness would anger Xerxes. But when her words were reported to the Persian king, he was pleased to hear a contradictory opinion, rather than the slavish agreement of sycophants. He valued her advice even more, but on this occasion he would not accept it. In a previous sea battle with the Greeks, the Persians had suffered, but he believed this was due to low morale resulting from his absence. This time he would overview the performance of his fleet and felt sure this would bring victory.

In her strategic advice, Artemisia may have added the fact that the channel between the island of Salamis and the Greek mainland was very narrow and so favoured the smaller numbers of the Greek navy. The huge forces of the Persian fleet would be throwing away their advantage. Xerxes probably realised this, but was determined to crush the Greek fleet to eliminate it as a threat to his intended invasion of the Peloponnese. With autumn storms approaching, the advance squadrons of his fleet set sail off Phaleron, hoping to attract the Greeks away from the straits of Salamis to the open water of the Saronic gulf. In the meantime, he sent a sizeable army towards the Peloponnese, in a move following Artemisia's suggestion that the Peloponnesian warriors in the Greek fleet would thus be encouraged to return home to defend their land.

Corinthian bronze helmet from about 490 BC and now in the State Collection of Classical Art, Munich.

Running short of supplies, just as Artemisia had identified, the Greeks on Salamis were becoming desperate. They were divided against each other and Themistocles, their commander, thought hard for some solution. In the end, he sent a message to Xerxes declaring that he had decided to commit his Athenian ships to the service of the Persian king, disgusted as he was by the selfish attitude of his former Peloponnesian allies. He told the king that the Peloponnesians were planning to leave Salamis at night to join their land forces and that Xerxes should attack them at once to prevent their escape.

Xerxes watching his mighty Persian army cross the Hellespont into Greece. From Cassell's *Universal History*, 1882.

56

Xerxes was tempted. The Persian fleet moved in and blockaded the straits of Salamis. The Peloponnesian break-out never came. Themistocles' message was a lie, intended to provoke the Persians. Artemisia's respect for the Greek fleet was well founded.

Early after dawn on 20 September 480 BC, Xerxes sat upon a gold throne and overlooked his ships. Strung across the narrow waters of the Salamis channel, they were arranged in a half-mile-wide front, with the Phoenicians on the right wing, the Ionian and Hellespontine Greeks of Asia Minor on the left, and contingents from Caria, Pamphylia, Lycia, Cilicia and Cyprus in the centre. Artemisia was not among the high command overlooking the fleet, but was actually on board one of her Halicarnassan triremes, commanding the ship's movements. Apparently, unlike the lighter Greek galleys, the Persian ships had high prows and sterns, being designed more for action in the open sea. Loaded with twice as many troops as the Greek ships—30 or 40 marines and archers to an Athenian crew of 14—the top-heavy nature of the Persian galleys decreased their manoeuvrability.

The battle began in confusion, with the majority of the Greek fleet sailing away from the Persians. The Persians pursued them, but as they chased the Athenian and Peloponnesian decoys into the narrower waters, a contingent of Aeginetans and Megarians bolted out from a bay to the immediate left of the Ionian triremes and smashed into them with their gleaming bronze-clad rams. In front of the Persians, the Athenian and Peloponnesian galleys turned in the shallow waters to face their pursuers. All the ships closed, slicing into each other, rams and oars becoming entangled, locking together so that their warriors could surge over their bows to slash and hack.

As the Persian ships crowded in, the wind rose and the waves swelled, rolling their overloaded vessels. The Athenians, in low-lying triremes, rode over the waves and preyed on the Persians as they tried to manoeuvre out of the crush. The Greeks sheared off their oars and then plunged into them broadside on. The Phoenicians were the first to break, running their ships aground. Before their king, they blamed their defeat on the Ionians, but Xerxes had observed the Ionians' strong resistance on the left wing and the lying Phoenicians were beheaded. The Greeks now surrounded the remaining Persian fleet as fishermen circle a shoal of fish.

Aeschylus, a Greek veteran of the conflict, describes the close combat from the point of view of the Persians: 'The hulls of our vessels rolled over and the sea was hidden from our sight, choked with wrecks and slaughtered men. The shores and reefs were strewn with corpses. In wild disorder, every ship remaining in our fleet turned tail and fled. But the Greeks pursued us, and with oars or broken fragments of wreckage struck the survivors' heads as though they were tunneys and a haul of fish. Shrieks and groans rang across the water until nightfall hid us from them.'

Artemisia was fortunate to still be in command of a functioning ship, but her luck was fast running out. Closely pursued by an Athenian galley, her escape to the open sea was blocked by Persian ships, each endeavouring to scrape past the other. With the imminent threat of a Greek assault on her stern, she quickly decided to surge on at full speed. Ahead, she spied the flagship of the Calyndian contingent, led by King Damasithymus. Calynda lay on the border of Lycia and Caria and it may well be that Artemisia held a personal grudge against the Calyndian king. Without giving any warning, Artemisia's ram splintered the ship with such an impact that it sank immediately, with few survivors. Seeing this dramatic action, the captain of the Greek ship pursuing Artemisia believed she must have been a friendly ship or a deserter from the Persians and so broke off his attack. Xerxes similarly misunderstood the target of Artemisia's attack and praised her for her aggression. 'My men have become women,' he growled at his commanders, 'and my women men.' Ameinias, the captain of the Greek ship that mistook Artemisia's identity, was furious when he learned the truth after the battle. The Athenians had offered a prize of 10,000 drachmas to any of their captains who brought back the head of the devilish woman. To them, Artemisia evoked the Amazon assault on Athens and they would defeat this invasion of Greece just as they had done that of the earlier warrior women.

The Greeks kept up their pursuit and destruction of the Persian fleet until sunset. The few remaining Persian vessels limped back to Phaleron. Xerxes had lost 200 ships against 40 Greek ships destroyed. The next morning, Themistocles, the Greek commander, awoke to the sounds of building across the straits of Salamis. Through the morning haze, he could see the Persians constructing a pontoon-bridge towards the island. He ordered his men on guard and prepared for a second attack. Meanwhile, Xerxes called his generals and advisers together. The naval defeat had profoundly shaken him and he was unsure what his next step should be. The construction work across the sea to Salamis was simply a ruse to give him more time to think, while keeping the Greeks on the defensive.

Within the war council, Mardonius, the chief Persian commander, realised the full extent of the disaster. He knew the fight had gone out of his army and, yet, the burden of defeat lay with him and he had to redeem himself in some way. He suggested that as Xerxes' land army remained invincible, it should advance against the Peloponnesians. Or, in a compromise that saved face and warriors, the majority of the army could return with Xerxes to Persia, while a picked forced stayed in Greece, giving Mardonius the opportunity to retrieve Persian pride. Xerxes was pleased with an idea that preserved himself and his court from further disaster, but left an occupying force on the Greek mainland. Before agreeing to Mardonius' compromise, he summoned Artemisia to the council. She alone had spoken out against the engagement at Salamis. Dismissing all his other advisers, he invited her to speak her mind.

All along, Artemisia had seen no virtue in a war against the Greeks and she certainly would not countenance any continuation of a major campaign

against the Peloponnesians. But even she could see that a general retreat would not be acceptable to the Persian king.

'It is difficult', she told Xerxes, 'to give a definite answer to what is best. But I would suggest that you march back, leaving Mardonius to whatever he promises. For if he does subdue the Greeks, then the achievement is yours. But if he fails, then it is no great loss to you, so long as your household is safe, for any Greek victory over Mardonius will not be a victory over you, but a defeat merely of one of your servants. As for you, you will march home having burnt Athens, the aim, after all, of your expedition.'

These were the words Xerxes wanted to hear. He had lost interest in the

Greek warriors preparing for battle. Artemisia's Halicarnassan warriors were similarly armed, the city-states of the eastern Aegean coast being long influenced by Greek culture. Detail from reverse of a calyx krater around 500 BC, now in the Metropolitan Museum of Art, New York.

campaign and wished to return safely to Persia; but by leaving Mardonius behind, he was keeping open the possibility of an honourable settlement. He thanked Artemisia for her wisdom and entrusted his sons to her. While he sailed to the Hellespont to oversee the return of his land army, she sailed directly to Ephesus. Thus ended the second Persian invasion of Greece. Mardonius did remain in Greece, but met with defeat and lost his life at the battle of Plataea. Xerxes returned to an empire racked with rebellion and conspiracy, of which he eventually became a victim. As for Artemisia, nothing is heard of her again. Presumably, from Ephesus she returned to Halicarnassus and continued to rule until her son could assume kingship. Her good relations with the Persian king must have assisted the prosperity of her dynasty and many wives of kings of Halicarnassus bore her name into the fourth century BC. It was one of these queens called Artemisia who built a magnificent tomb at Halicarnassus for her husband, Mausolus—one of the seven wonders of the ancient world. Among the sumptuous decoration on the building was a marble frieze depicting Amazons battling against Greeks, with the Amazons seemingly having the best of the combat—an echo of Artemisia's naval prowess.

Throughout the ancient Mediterranean, there are several occasions when women assumed power on the death of their husbands. Many more were content to wield influence behind the scenes, becoming formidable power-brokers for their husbands and children. All maintained substantial private bodyguards for the occasions when reasoned politics broke down into open conflict. But few emerged on to the battlefield to lead their armies in campaigns of aggression against other rulers. One of the most celebrated of these women warlords in the Roman world was Zenobia, Queen of Palmyra.

In 1874, Dr William Wright headed a small expedition out of Damascus along the desert tracks of the Syrian plain in search of Zenobia's lost kingdom. It was a journey undertaken by few Europeans. Bedouin bandits regularly raided caravans crossing the desert. On 1 June, accompanied by armed horsemen, Wright obtained his first view of the ancient ruins of Palmyra. 'After the bare monotonous desert,' he wrote, 'we come gradually on a source of enchantment, and though we have come expressly to see the scene, it breaks upon us as a surprise; not all at once, but increasing at every step—castle and tower and temple, and serried lines of Corinthian capitals, seen in part, and in such a way as to suggest more, lead up with the most dramatic effect to the most splendid denouement. The thrill of expectancy and delight is a rich reward for all our fatigue.'

As he rode on, Wright came to the colossal remains of the Sanctuary of Bel. Inside its walls he saw rows of clay-daubed huts inhabited by nomadic Arabs. 'Wherever we go among these human dens there reek filth and squalor and the hot pestiferous atmosphere of an ill-kept stye. Such is now the state of that gorgeous temple.' Seventeen hundred years previously, the temple had been but one of many remarkable buildings and fine houses that made Palmyra one of the most splendid cities of the ancient Near East. At

the centre of a trade route carrying goods from the Mediterranean across the desert to the Persian Gulf, it had grown rich and attractive under Roman patronage. It was within the walls of this jewel among the sands in the third century AD that Zenobia learnt the business of power and how to exercise it.

Septimia Zenobia, the Latinised form of the Aramaic name Bat Zabbai, was a woman of distinct physical appearance and strong personality. 'Her face was dark and of a swarthy hue,' wrote a Roman chronicler in the fourth-century *Historia Augusta*. 'Her eyes were black and powerful, her spirit divinely great, and her beauty incredible. So white were her teeth that many thought she had pearls in place of them. Her voice was clear and like that of a man. Her sternness, when necessity demanded, was that of a tyrant; her clemency, when her sense of right called for it, that of a good emperor.'

It may have been Zenobia's beauty that first brought her to the attention of Odaenathus, ruler of Palmyra, but it was most certainly her character and intelligence that kept her close to his side throughout his reign. She was not content to remain within her husband's palace, but accompanied the warlord as adviser as well as wife. At first hand, she learnt the reality of politics and warfare. 'She rarely made use of a woman's coach, but more often rode a horse,' records the *Historia Augusta*. 'Sometimes she walked with her footsoldiers for several miles. She hunted with the eagerness of a

Spaniard, often drank with her generals, and sometimes drank with Persians and Armenians to get the better of them. As servants she had eunuchs of advanced age and very few maidens.' Her intelligence was considerable, too. Aside from her native Aramaic tongue, she spoke Egyptian and read Greek. Her knowledge of the history of Alexandria led her at one stage to write a short account of the Orient and she frequently claimed to be descended from the family of Cleopatra. Such a belief may have fuelled her future ambitions.

Odaenathus, Zenobia's husband, was a bold opportunist. When the Emperor Valerian was captured by the Persian ruler Shapur I in 260, there was a strong possibility that the whole eastern Roman empire would fall to the dynamic warriors of the newly rising Persian Sasanid dynasty. Odaenathus, son of a ruling family in Palmyra and recipient of the imperial rank of *Consularis*, assumed the defence of the entire Asian provinces of the Roman Empire against the Persian threat. If he succeeded, then his position in the Near East would be unchallengeable and although he had the good sense to acknowledge the seniority of the emperor, he would, in reality, rule as an independent lord of the prosperous Roman provinces of the Near East. It was too great a chance to miss.

With the money of his family, the Julii Aurelii Septimii, backing him, Odaenathus recruited his own troops and added them to the remains of a Roman army in Syria. With Zenobia riding at his side, he set out in late 260 against the Persian king. Marching towards the River Euphrates, he defeated the Persian army and recaptured the city of Nisibis, pursuing Shapur as far as Ctesiphon on the River Tigris. Having secured Mesopotamia, Odaenathus went on to crush a rebellion against the Roman emperor. A grateful empire made him *Restitutor totius Orientis*, governor of all Roman provinces in the east, from Asia Minor to Egypt, a title previously borne only by emperors. In response, Odaenathus proclaimed himself King of Palmyra, the first in his family.

For seven years, Odaenathus ruled the Roman East with an iron command. The Persian Sasanids were humbled and the Roman Empire could concentrate on defending its European borders against the barbarians. Throughout this period, Zenobia supported and embellished her husband's lordship. Under her guidance, several prominent artists and writers were invited to the Palmyrene court, among them the Greek philosopher Cassius Longinus. But Zenobia and Odaenathus also shared an enjoyment of hunting and other outdoor activities. 'From his earliest years,' says the *Historia Augusta*, 'Odaenathus expended his sweat in taking lions, panthers and bears living in the forest and mountains, enduring heat and rain and all the other hardships and pleasures which hunting entails. Hardened by these he was able to bear the sun and the dust in the wars with the Persians. And his wife too was inured to hardship and in the opinion of many was braver than her husband.'

From what little evidence we have, it appears that Zenobia and

Parthian terracotta of a mounted archer. When Zenobia ruled Palmyra, the Parthian Empire had only recently collapsed and her army was heavily influenced by it. Possibly third century AD, found in Syria.

Odaenathus enjoyed an unusually close and equal relationship for such a powerful ruler in the ancient Near East. With this in mind, it seems strange that Zenobia should conspire to his assassination in 267. According to the *Historia Augusta*, the motive for this suggestion lies in Zenobia's fear that Herodes, Odaenathus' eldest son would succeed him. Herodes was his father's son by a previous marriage and was, by all accounts, a worthless and spoilt boy for whom Zenobia had little time. The instrument of Odaenathus' murder was his cousin Maeonius, who was shortly after killed by Zenobia's soldiers. The only evidence to suggest that Zenobia was involved in this plot was the sudden disappearance of her stepson, Herodes, immediately after his father's death. Thereafter, Vaballathus, Zenobia's young son, was proclaimed successor to the Palmyrene crown, but until he was old enough to rule, Zenobia would act as regent. Zosimus, the other chief chronicler of Zenobia, makes no reference at all to her being guilty of her husband's murder. He simply states that Odaenathus lost his life in a conspiracy while he was celebrating the birthday of a friend. Zenobia then took over his affairs with the assistance of her husband's friends. In this, there is no suggestion of a *coup d'état*, but more the defeat of an attempted take-over followed by a resumption of rule by the Septimii dynasty.

Zenobia was too forceful a personality to allow her family's political ambitions to stagnate. Shortly after her assumption of power, her advisers brought her an invitation. It came from an Egyptian called Timagenes. Little is known about him, except that he must have held considerable military and political power in Egypt. Dissatisfied with the rule of the Romans, he asked Zenobia to intervene and take direct control of Egyptian affairs. It was an opportunity Odaenathus would have leapt at and Zenobia was inclined to pursue it. The main danger was that it was an act of aggression, placing Palmyra in open confrontation with the Roman Empire. Encouraged by her advisers, Zenobia considered the prize of the Nile worth it.

While Zenobia planned her Egyptian campaign, another threat to the security of the Roman Near East was defeated. This time, it was not the Persians but a marauding fleet of Goth pirates from the Black Sea. They raided Greece and Asia Minor and were only dispersed after a tough campaign led by the Emperor Claudius. With the immediate threat to her Asian dominions over, and the likely exhaustion of the Roman military leadership, Zenobia considered the time right to push ahead with her invasion of Egypt. She sent her general Zabdas at the head of an army, said to number 70,000 consisting of Palmyrenes, Syrians and Arab barbarians. At this stage, there is no evidence that Zenobia actually accompanied her army on the expedition.

Once within Egyptian territory, Zabdas was joined by an Egyptian army led by Timagenes. Together, they defeated a 50,000-strong Roman-Egyptian army. Not wishing to risk his soldiers any further, Zabdas hastily established Timagenes as representative of the Palmyrene party in Egypt and returned homewards, leaving a garrison of 5,000 troops. Hearing of this insult to Roman dominion, the Emperor Claudius dispatched his admiral Probus to Alexandria. Egypt was always a highly sensitive region to the Romans. They received much of their grain shipments from the Nile and any domination of this market could seriously affect its price and disrupt the Roman economy. Experienced at combating the Goth pirates, Probus had a war-hardened force beneath him. In two rapid conflicts, Probus forced the Palmyrenes out of Egypt. Timagenes rallied and in a surprise attack, with only 2,000 men, thoroughly defeated Probus on a desert mountain-top somewhere between Egypt and Palmyra. Despite having misjudged the strength of Roman opposition, Zenobia's Egyptian expedition had ended in success, with a ruler loyal to her in power. The possibility of establishing an empire of the Near East to rival that of the Romans could not have escaped her.

The relative ease of Zenobia's campaign in Egypt encouraged her to send an army northwards and march east through Asia Minor, establishing her

Sasanid silver dish showing Shapur II hunting. The new Persian dynasty was another strong military influence on Zenobia. Early fourth century AD, now in the British Museum, London.

authority in Ankara and as far as Chalcedon, on the opposite shore of the Bosporus to Contantinople. Her rule over Bithynia was short-lived. As soon as its people heard news of the creation of a new emperor in 270, they threw off Palmyrene domination. It was not the mere fact of a new Roman emperor that gave them the courage, but the news that it was Aurelian: only he was strong enough to contest Zenobia's hold on Asia.

Born of a modest Illyrian family in the Balkans, Aurelian was a professional soldier. An excellent cavalry commander, he had fought with such vigour against the northern barbarians that there were few to dispute his succession to the imperial rank. Immediately on receiving power, he ruthlessly set about crushing all rebellions and barbarian incursions. His reputation travelled before him to Asia Minor. As soon as he set foot in the Orient, rebels fled and cities opened their gates to him. Before the walls of Tyana in Cappadocia, the 55-year-old warrior emperor declared: 'In this city I shall not leave one dog alive.' Knowing this signalled an unbridled orgy of plunder and destruction if they captured the city, his soldiers fought all the harder. Fearing the worst, one citizen lost his nerve and opened the gates to the ferocious conqueror. At once, Aurelian responded

Aurelian, Roman Emperor between 270 and 275 AD, Zenobia's chief adversary. Drawing from a Roman coin of the third century AD.

with a decision that earned him the respect of the Asian population and Roman chroniclers. Rather than succumbing to the base instincts of his warriors, Aurelian risked their wrath by denying the plunder they wanted. Instead, to justify his original promise, he explained: 'I did indeed declare that I would not leave a dog alive in the city. Well then, kill all the dogs.' Such was the loyalty of his troops that they took up the good humour of their leader and accepted a more civilised reward. The whole of Asia Minor breathed more easily after this display of clemency. Aurelian was a human warlord. This made Zenobia's task of resisting the emperor all the more difficult.

By this time, the fame of Zenobia's leadership had spread throughout the Roman world. Her reputation as an 'iron lady' ensured that many writers described her in Amazonian terms. 'It is said,' repeats the historian Trebellius Pollio, 'that she would only sleep with her husband for the purpose of conception. She would sleep with him once and then refrain until the time of menstruation to see if she was pregnant. If not, she would then grant him another opportunity of begetting a child.' With such mythical descriptions enhancing her image as a stern warlord, it was becoming clear that any confrontation between her and Aurelian would be titanic. Equally charismatic, equally ambitious, the deciding confrontation was fast-approaching.

Not letting any time slip by, Aurelian rapidly marched on Antioch on the Syrian coast. There, a Palmyrene army blocked his advance beyond the River Orontes, just outside the city. Aurelian carefully noted the composition of his enemy. Heavily influenced by the Parthians and Sasanid Persians, the Palmyrenes were largely cavalry and the most formidable of these were heavily armoured horsemen, called *cataphracti* or *clibanarii*: clad head to foot in mail and plate, even their horses were coated in scale armour. In a sixth-century Persian list of armaments required by each *cataphractus* on parade, the chronicler Tabari describes fully their personal armoury: mail, breastplate, helmet, leg-guards, arm-guards, horse-armour, lance, buckler, sword, mace, battleaxe, quiver of 30 arrows, bowcase with two bows, and two separate bowstrings. Confronted by such human tanks, it is little wonder that Aurelian placed his infantry safely on one side of the river, beyond the enemy cavalry. He then ordered his horsemen on the other side not to engage with the armoured cavalry, but to retreat before their charge.

According to Zosimus, Aurelian's tactics worked. His Roman cavalry made a controlled retreat before the Palmyrene *clibanarii* to the village of Immae, eastwards along the road from Antioch. When the Romans saw the heavily armoured Palmyrenes were tired by the pursuit, they suddenly wheeled round and cut down the exhausted horsemen. This first clash compelled the remaining Palmyrene warriors to retreat within the walls of Antioch. Fearing that this defeat would encourage the citizens of Antioch to turn on their Palmyrene overlords, Zabdas, Zenobia's leading general, endeavoured to trick them into submission. He mounted one of his warriors upon a horse dressed in similar clothes to the Roman emperor's. Leading the disguised man through the streets of Antioch, he convinced the citizens he had captured Aurelian. Such a ruse was intended only to buy him time. Under cover of night, he slipped out of the city and led the remnants of his vanguard to Emesa, where Zenobia was awaiting news of his success.

In Aurelian's treatment of the citizens of Antioch, it becomes clear that his aim in this campaign was not punishment but reconciliation. When he entered the city, he was told that much of its population had fled. In response, he published edicts throughout the city and countryside saying that the people of Antioch had had no choice in their submission to Zenobia and that subsequently he bore them no ill will. With this guarantee, the fugitives returned to the city. It was Aurelian's policy of clemency throughout this campaign that proved his single most important strategy. By winning the hearts and minds of the people of the Near East, he ensured a quick advance through enemy territory. But this still left the problem of Zenobia's considerable armed forces. The army he had overthrown at Antioch was probably only a large vanguard. The body of Zenobia's army remained undefeated somewhere south along the River Orontes.

Shaken by Zabdas' defeat, it seems likely that Zenobia decided to lead her warriors in person. To see their queen on the battlefield would give the Palmyrenes the fire in their heart they needed to defeat the Romans. With the survivors of Zabdas's vanguard and her own body of fresh troops, Zenobia resolved to face Aurelian outside the desert town of Emesa, now called Homs. With the mountains of Lebanon to the west and the arid plains of Syria to the east, it straddled the caravan route to her capital at Palmyra. Aurelian must pass no further.

When sweating scouts broke into Zenobia's headquarters at Emesa with news of Aurelian's approach, the warrior queen ordered armour to be brought to her. A tunic of mail was placed over her silk underclothes. Over this hung purple drapery, symbolic of her claim to imperial power. The cloth was secured with a large jewelled brooch. The brooch was a military and regal emblem, not a piece of jewellery. On her head she wore a helmet, perhaps of Roman design or Persian. Her arms remained bare, cooling her armoured body beneath the glaring desert sun. Outside her headquarters, she mounted a horse and in the company of Zabdas and her generals rode out to the city of tents housing her warriors. Around 70,000 warriors assembled before her. The majority of the army were horsemen and the core of them Zenobia's élite *clibanarii*, proud noblemen with the finest arms and armour money could buy. Around them were hordes of nomadic Arab horsemen, lightly armoured but excellent archers. Recruited mainly from the gangs of Syrian bandits that terrorised the caravan routes, they were tough, battle-hardened warriors, no less fierce than their more heavily armoured partners. The *clibanarii* were motivated by loyalty to Zenobia's regime and their own aristocratic arrogance. The Arab horsemen were interested in only one thing—loot. It was a formidable combination. To this were added a few companies of foot-soldiers, useful as points of stability and defence, but most likely recruited from the local Lebanese-Syrian population and not wholly trustworthy.

Aurelian was on a winning streak, but was realistic enough to know he faced his greatest challenge in battling Zenobia in person. His army may have been smaller in numbers, but it was of good morale. Among the professional Roman legionaries he brought from Europe were contingents from Dalmatia (cavalry), Moesia, Pannonia, as well as Celtic legionaries from Noricum and Rhaetia. To these were added Moorish horsemen and warriors recruited from Tyana, Mesopotamia, Syria, Phoenicia and Palestine. Having decided on his plan of battle, Aurelian awaited the thunderous roll of the

Funerary relief bust of a Palmyrene noblewoman of the second century AD, now in the British Museum, London.

enemy cavalry. Knowing the strength of her horsemen wilted with each hour beneath the rising sun, Zenobia signalled a general advance of her cavalry. The Arabs sprang forward first, throwing javelins and shooting arrows at the Roman lines. Behind them rumbled the *clibanarii*, searching for a gap through which to smash the Romans' resolve.

Fearing encirclement, Aurelian tried to repeat the tactics that brought him success at Antioch. He ordered his cavalry to retreat before the Palmyrenes and exhaust them by the time they reached his lines of foot-soldiers. Such a difficult manoeuvre, highly dependent on rigid discipline, proved too much for the Roman cavalry. Feeling the Arab horsemen hard at their heels, their orderly retreat broke into a panic and their formations dissolved. Zenobia rode forward with her generals. Anticipating victory, the *clibanarii* spurred their armoured horses into a trot and then a charge. The Roman cavalry collapsed before them, speared and hacked by their lances and battleaxes.

With Roman bodies strewn around them, the Palmyrene cavalry assumed victory. It was true: the Roman cavalry were scattered and in no condition to offer a threat. But among the clouds of dust remained Aurelian's formations of foot-soldiers. Somewhat awed by the spectacle of thousands of Palmyrene horsemen, they were nevertheless under the control of his officers and ready for battle. With the Palmyrene cavalry recklessly pursuing individual enemies across the desert, Aurelian ordered his warriors to advance in close formation. With the Palmyrene lines broken and some believing the battle was over, they fell easy prey to the companies of Roman foot-soldiers methodically surrounding and dispatching gangs of Palmyrene horsemen. The Palestinians were particularly adept at this. Armed with long clubs studded with nails and iron spikes, the agile Palestinians smashed the exhausted *clibanarii* from their saddles. The Palmyrene noblemen were battered to a pulp within their coats of brass-decorated iron mail.

Hearing the shrieks of death and defeat, and seeing her warriors stumbling out of the desert dust in disarray, Zenobia realised her dream of victory was over. Her advisers told her to retreat before she was overrun by the emperor's troops. But where could she run? The citizens of Emesa were no longer friendly to her, interested only in establishing terms with the winner of the conflict beyond their walls. There was no time to waste. Zenobia and her generals turned their horses towards Palmyra, leaving a considerable treasure within the walls of Emesa as Aurelian's prize.

Aurelian was received with great celebration by the citizens of Emesa, who had heard of his fair temper. But the campaign was still not over. Pausing only to rest his troops and horses, Aurelian was soon hot on the trail of the Palmyrene queen, across the desert tracks of the Syrian plains. This time, his advance was not so easy. Throughout, he was attacked by bands of Arab nomads, furious at his defeat of their tribesmen at Emesa. When he finally reached the outskirts of Palmyra, the task of assaulting the city was no less daunting. From archaeological evidence at the site of Palmyra today, it appears that the city in Zenobia's time was surrounded by two walls. The outermost covered a vast area but may only have been a low wall delineating the limits of orchards and fields on the city's edge. The inner wall, called Zenobia's Wall, enclosed her palace and the principal civic buildings, as well as a concentrated residential area containing many of the palaces of the wealthy Palmyrenes. This was a tall barrier of large stone blocks strengthened by towers and bastions.

In a letter to a friend, Aurelian revealed his doubts about breaking Palmyra's defences. 'There are Romans who say that I am waging a war against a mere woman,' he wrote, 'but there is as great an army before me as though I were fighting a man. I cannot tell you what a great store of arrows,

spears, and stones is here, what great preparations they have made. There is
no section of the wall that is not held by two or three engines of war. Their
machines even hurl fire. What else can I say? She fears like a woman and
fights as one who fears punishment. But I believe that the gods will bring
aid to the Roman Empire because they have not failed us yet.'

Riding around the city's defences, Aurelian searched for a point at which

71

to begin his assault. While he surveyed the walls, Palmyrene citizens leant over the battlements and shouted cries of defiance. One citizen in particular hurled abuse of an indecent and personal nature at the emperor. Aurelian's personal bodyguard was outraged at this. 'Will you grant me permission to silence that insolent man?' a Persian guard asked Aurelian. The emperor agreed and the Persian raised a powerful bow. With one shot, the bodyguard struck the citizen midway through a tirade of insults so his body fell over the battlements before the emperor. It was considered a good omen, but the siege dragged on and on. The Palmyrenes had a good supply of food and the Romans were in greater danger of starvation and disease. Aurelian tried to reason with the warrior queen and sent her a letter.

'From Aurelian, Emperor of the Roman world and recoverer of the East, to Zenobia and all others who are bound to her by alliance in war. You should have done of your own free will what I now command in my letter. I bid you to surrender, promising that your lives shall be spared with the condition that you, Zenobia, together with your children shall live wherever I, acting in accordance with the wish of the most noble senate, shall appoint a place. Your jewels, gold, silver, silks, horses, and camels shall be handed over to the Roman treasury. As for the people of Palmyra, their rights shall be preserved.'

Zenobia was furious. Aurelian addressed her with no reference to her illustrious title, her right through Odaenathus to rule the Roman Near East. It was a call for unconditional surrender. She could never accept it. Dictating her answer in Syrian, but having it written in Greek, she replied with complete faith in eventual victory.

'From Zenobia, Queen of the East, to Aurelian Augustus. None save yourself has ever demanded by letter what you now demand. Whatever must be accomplished in matters of war must be done by valour alone. You demand my surrender as though you were not aware that Cleopatra preferred to die a Queen rather than remain alive, however high her rank. At this very moment, we are expecting reinforcements from Persia. On our side also are the Arabs and Armenians. The bandits of Syria have defeated your army, Aurelian. What more need be said? When these forces arrive, you will surely lay aside the arrogance with which you demand my surrender.'

Secretly, Zenobia and her advisers were not so confident. There was no indication of any reinforcements from the Persians. At a council of her generals, a repeated request was made for Sasanid help. Since receiving Zenobia's letter of defiance, Aurelian had intensified his efforts to take the city by force. Each day, his siege machines chipped away at the massive walls. His miners burrowed into the desert earth. In the Palmyrene council, the situation was declared serious enough for Zenobia's generals to recommend she leave the city and ride to the Persian Empire. Under cover of night, Zenobia rode a dromedary camel into the dark, accompanied by only a few bodyguards.

When Aurelian heard of Zenobia's flight, he was enraged and sent his fastest Arab horsemen in pursuit of her. Despite the speed of her camel, the horsemen closed the gap. As she prepared to cross the River Euphrates into Persia, the Roman horsemen appeared out of the dust and seized her. Zenobia's reign was at an end. Hearing the news of her capture, the citizens of Palmyra made peace terms with Aurelian and surrendered the city. Aurelian treated them well and respected their rights. Leaving a garrison at Palmyra, Aurelian took Zenobia and her courtiers to Emesa and put them on trial for their crimes against the empire.

'Why did you dare to show such insolence to the emperors of Rome?' Aurelian asked her.

'You, I accept, are an Emperor,' she replied, 'because you win victories. But your predecessors I have never regarded as worthy of the Emperorship. I desired to become a partner in the royal power, should there be enough land.'

At the end of her hearing, Zenobia blamed her actions on the bad advice of her counsellors, naming the Greek philosopher Longinus as a chief influence. As a result of her testimony, Longinus and several other distinguished courtiers were executed. The relish with which this story is told by the Roman chroniclers suggests an attempt to present Zenobia as a wicked woman full of female weakness and vindictiveness. In contrast to this is the virtual eulogy made by Aurelian to the Senate.

'I have heard', he declared, 'that men are reproaching me for having performed an unmanly deed in leading Zenobia in triumph. But in truth, those very persons who find fault with me now would accord me praise in abundance did they but know what manner of woman she is, how wise in counsel, how steadfast in plans, how firm toward soldiers, how generous when necessity calls, and how stern when discipline demands. I might even say that it was her who enabled Odaenathus to defeat the Persians and, after putting Shapur to flight, advanced all the way to Ctesiphon. I might add also that such was the fear that this woman inspired in the peoples of the East and also the Egyptians, Arabs, and Armenians, that none ever moved against her. Nor would I have spared her life had I not known that she did a great service to the Roman state when she preserved the imperial power in the East for herself and her children.'

With reluctance, almost, did Aurelian move against Zenobia, for a powerful Palmyra was a useful buffer against the Persian state. There was another reason for Aurelian sparing Zenobia's life. He wanted to crown his victories in the empire by leading her in a triumphal parade through the streets of Rome. On the morning of Aurelian's parade, Zenobia was carefully prepared to reflect the wealth and splendour of her Oriental court. She was laden with jewels so heavy that she faltered under their weight. Her feet and hands were bound with gold chains and around her neck was a gold chain held by a Persian clown. She was then led on to a chariot decorated with silver, gold and jewels, which she herself had had made in the belief that one day she would visit Rome as a victor. Instead, she was carried in it as but one prize in the emperor's magnificent booty. Aurelian rode in a chariot drawn by four stags. Advancing to the Capitol, he headed a spectacular procession: 20 elephants and 200 wild beasts, including tigers, giraffes and elks; 800 pairs of gladiators and prisoners from Arabia, India, Africa, Bactria and Persia; barbarians, including Goths, Alans, Sarmatians, Franks, Suebians and Vandals; and 10 women, clad in armour, who had been captured with the Goths—placards carried before them declared they were Amazons. Then came the gilded chariots bearing Tetricus, a rebellious Gaul, in scarlet cloak and Celtic trousers, and Zenobia, laden with jewels and gold chains. Together they represented Aurelian's triumph over both western and eastern enemies of the empire. The crowd was hysterical, enthralled by the material splendour and military might. Zenobia's chariot was followed by servants, holding aloft gold crowns presented by all the cities the emperor had captured. Then came Roman dignitaries, guildsmen and horsemen clad in mail, soldiers and senators at the tail. The procession took all day to pass by the Capitol. Aurelian declared a holiday and the people of Rome were given bread, meat and gladiatorial games. None could contest Aurelian's supreme power.

With the cheers and jeers of the Roman crowd ringing in her ears, Zenobia must have returned to her quarters on the evening of the triumph with suicide in her mind. Cleopatra had long been her guiding model and now she considered the Egyptian queen's final gesture. Such a crisis must have passed, for the Roman chronicler Trebellius Pollio claims that Zenobia married a Roman nobleman and spent the rest of her life at a villa near Tivoli, just outside Rome. Her descendants also were recorded as living in Rome. It seems likely that Zenobia's very notoriety may have accorded her some celebrity status among the Roman aristocracy, who loved to hear anecdotes of a Palmyrene Empire in the desert while they sipped their wine in the comfort of a dinner-party.

Celtic Queens

MEDB, CARTIMANDUA, AND BOUDICA

One night, lying in bed together, Medb of Connacht took exception to her husband's boasting.

'It is fortunate you married me,' he said. 'You are so much better off now.'

'I was well enough off without you,' she retorted.

'All I heard of was a few womanish trinkets and the loot your enemies took away from you.'

Medb sat up in bed and glared at the man next to her.

'I am the daughter of the high king of Ireland. I had fifteen hundred warriors in my household and for every paid soldier I had ten more. My father gave me the entire western region of Ireland. My dowry brought you gold and chariots. If anyone has cause for upset, it is I, for you are a kept man.'

Her husband, Ailill of Leinster, leapt out of bed and stabbed his finger at her.

'That is ridiculous. None has more property and jewels than I. As for your realm, I have never heard of one ruled by a woman. That is why I took the kingship here.'

To prove each other's point, all their precious possessions were brought to the royal bedroom: jewellery, nuggets of gold, beautiful textiles, and fine pots and plates. But it was not enough. They went out to view their finest livestock. Stallions, rams, prize boars and cattle were paraded. Their wealth was equal on every count except one: Ailill had a mighty bull brought before the queen. Medb had no animal to match this. She called for time to find a bull to compete with her husband's and sent a messenger to Ulster, where she had heard of a particularly fine animal. She would borrow it and settle the quarrel. But the Ulstermen refused to give up such a great treasure—the Brown Bull of Cuailnge. It was a matter of pride and only force of arms could make the bull leave Ulster.

When Medb and Ailill heard the refusal of the Ulstermen, they resolved together to teach the haughty northerners a lesson and steal the bull. A marital argument would end in war. An army gathered from all Ireland. Each of Ailill's six brothers brought 3,000 warriors. Three thousand Ulster exiles joined the venture, forming three companies under the leadership of Cormac. The first company had their hair shorn, wore tunics down to their knees and speckled cloaks wrapped round their bodies. They carried long shields and broad, grey, stabbing spears. The second company wore slate-grey cloaks and red-embroidered tunics. Their hair was tied at the back of their heads and they wielded brightly coloured shields and five-pronged spears. The third company wore purple cloaks with red-embroidered, hooded tunics down to their feet. Their hair hung to their shoulders and they carried curved, scallop-edged shields and thick, shafted spears.

At the head of the army stood Medb in her chariot.

'Everyone leaving a wife or a sister today will curse me,' she said, 'For this army fights for me.'

She then led the Celtic army on a route north-eastwards from her capital at Cruachan, in Connacht, to Cuailnge, in Ulster. According to the *Tain Bo Cuailnge*, the ancient Irish source for this story, Medb was the chief military leader of the expedition, although all decisions seem to have been discussed with Ailill and the other Irish kings present. As they advanced into enemy territory, Medb gained word of her main adversary, an heroic warrior called Cuchulainn.

'What sort of man is he?' she asked.

'He is 17 years old,' replied Fergus, one of her generals. 'But there is no harder warrior in Ulster. There is no animal more fierce or hungry for flesh. In fury, splendour, voice, and physical power, there is none like Cuchulainn. Only he has achieved the battle-feat of nine men on each point.'

Medb was unimpressed.

'There is too much talk about him. He has but one body and he too is vulnerable to wounding like all of us.'

Riding deeper into Ulster, Medb and her army were confronted by cut-down trees, blocking their path. On the tree trunks were inscribed ogam (an ancient alphabet) messages challenging them to certain feats. If they failed to jump an oak trunk in a chariot or some other feat, then Cuchulainn would slay a chief warrior. Even Medb came under attack from the Ulster hero's slingshot. A stone killed the pet squirrel sitting on her shoulder. But still Medb rode on, with her warriors' shields raised high around her head.

As they entered the land of Cuailnge, Ailill became suspicious of the close relations between Medb and Fergus, her chief warrior and exiled Ulster-man. One of his spies witnessed them sleeping together and stole the sword of Fergus.

'That is all right,' Aililled told the spy. 'Medb sleeps with Fergus to keep his support on our expedition, but give me his sword. At least I can laugh at its theft.'

No more was heard of the indiscretion and Medb continued with the campaign. To stop Cuchulainn harassing her army day and night, she sent

Complete Celtic bronze
shield, the only one of its
kind found in Europe.
Discovered in a gravel pit in
Chertsey, Surrey, in 1985,
now in the British Museum,
London.

several of her bravest warriors against him in single combat. Every one of them failed even to wound the Ulsterman. In their turn, they were split from head to navel by one mighty blow of his sword. Medb and Ailill offered wine and a beautiful woman to any man who would face Cuchulainn. Many more did, but all perished. Medb admitted that Cuchulainn could never be conquered in fair combat and offered him a truce. The Ulster hero was to come unarmed to Focherd hill. There, Medb and her female attendants would meet with him to talk peace. Cuchulainn agreed to the meeting, but his charioteer advised him to carry his sword.

'Medb is a cunning woman,' he said, 'and a warrior without a weapon ceases to be governed by the laws of chivalry. He can be treated as a coward and cut down.'

As Cuchulainn rode up the slope of Focherd, he could see Medb on horseback, with her maidens in attendance. As he drew closer, armed warriors sprang from the bushes and surrounded him. Fourteen javelins left their hands, but none broke his skin. Outraged at the treachery, Cuchulainn's body shook and muscles swelled inside him, changing his appearance, peeling back the flesh on his face to reveal the bones and fangs of a fighting man. His enemies called him the Warped One. With the blade-sharp rim of his shield, he spun among the warriors and felled them like a cyclone. Medb's fists tingled with frustration and horror. Cuchulainn was superhuman.

Medb sent more men out to combat Cuchulainn, some singly, some in groups. She even offered herself as a prize. Throughout the *Tain*, she uses her sexuality as a tool to rouse her warriors and defeat Cuchulainn. But, inevitably, the time was coming close when the combat could only be settled by one final battle: a titanic duel between Cuchulainn and the warriors of Ulster against Medb and her Irish army from the three other provinces. The warriors gathered on a plain beneath Slemain Midi. All the champions on each side rode up in their chariots at the head of their company of warriors. Medb rode before her men, inspiring them with her appearance—a tall, blonde, long-faced woman with soft features. Two gold birds sat on her shoulders. A purple cloak was wrapped around her, secured by a brilliant gold brooch. In one hand she held a light, throwing spear. In the other, she gripped an iron sword.

On the day of the battle, Cuchulainn was exhausted by wounds and the exertion of battling some of the greatest champions in Ireland. He asked his charioteer to describe the events of the day. Before sunrise, herdsmen from the Ulster camp went in pursuit of stray animals. As they searched for cattle, they fell among servants from Medb's camp and fighting broke out. While the sun shimmered above the horizon, the noise of the battle roused the warriors of both camps. They rushed naked into the conflict. With each new hour of the sun, more and more warriors rose to join the battle. Their chariots hurtled across the plain, breaking each other's lines. Medb held back some of her chariots in case she needed to pluck Ailill from danger.

Celtic women defend their wagons against the Roman assault at Aquae Sextiae. Romantic, late-nineteenth century engraving.

Medb asked Fergus to join the battle, but he protested he had lost his sword and carried one made only of wood. Ailill's resentment of the champion's dalliance with his wife relented and he sent for Fergus's sword.

'With that blade,' Ailill said, 'lay Ulster low.'

Fergus seized the weapon in both hands and charged among the Ulstermen, swathing a great gap among them, slaying a hundred. In the turmoil, a warrior called Conall Cernach taunted him.

'You rage hard at your fellow Ulstermen,' he yelled. 'All for the sake of a whore's backside.'

On these words, Medb urged her chariot forward and crashed into the crowd of warriors, hurling her javelin into the struggling flesh. At her side rode her seven sons and nine troops of 3,000 men. Fergus struck at everything around him. When Conchobor, chief of the Ulstermen, confronted him, Fergus brought his double-handed sword down on his shield with such a ringing blow that Cuchulainn heard it from his place of rest.

'Unleash me from my sick-bed,' the hero cried. A battle spasm stiffened his body and he leapt to his chariot.

'I'll churn you up like foam in a whirlpool,' he boomed to Fergus. 'Remember the promise we swore when last we met.'

Fergus shivered with rage. In an earlier encounter, he had persuaded the Ulster hero to back away from him, so that neither mighty champion should taste each other's blood. But Cuchulainn only agreed if Fergus would do the same when next they met. Now was the time. Bound by his word, Fergus rode away from the battle, taking with him his 3,000 warriors. With him went the men of Munster and Galeoin, leaving Medb and Ailill to continue the battle. It was noon, and Cuchulainn rode his chariot into the main conflict, smashing into everyone before him, holding myriad heads in each hand. Medb ordered a rearguard to raise a wall of shields. She sent the captured Brown Bull of Cuailnge, the prize of the whole endeavour, back to Cruachan under a separate escort, so that if no one survived the battle, at least the bull would have been captured as she had sworn. Then Medb felt the need to relieve herself. It was the time of her period and her bloody urine stained the earth behind the wall of shields. At her most vulnerable, Cuchulainn cornered her, but he would not strike. The battle was over and he allowed Medb to retreat with her remaining warriors.

'It has been a sad and sorry day,' Medb sighed to Fergus.

'It is not surprising for a herd led by a mare to stray and destroy itself,' he replied. 'We should not have followed the rump of a misguided woman.'

The *Tain* ends with a battle between the Bull of Cuailnge and the great Bull of Ailill. Naturally, the Bull of Cuailnge is victorious, but as it returned to Ulster, it fell dead from exhaustion. Medb and Ailill made peace with Cuchulainn and no Irishman died in fighting for seven years.

The *Tain Bo Cuailnge* says much about Celtic attitudes to women warlords. It is not thought strange that a woman should head an army. Indeed, such a woman can be bold, clever and physically brave. But ultimately, her female physique lacks the endurance to bring her success. Medb's menstruating is the symbol chosen for this innate female weakness. It is a universal taboo traditionally held by men who argue that women cannot bear arms. A menstruating woman in many primitive societies is considered an ill omen before battle and should not be allowed to touch weapons.

Among the majority of Celtic women, a supporting role in warfare appears to have been the norm, preparing the camp and provisions of their warriors. Sometimes, unavoidably, these women were embroiled in the fighting. The most famous examples of this occurred during the invasion of southern France by the Cimbric and Teutones tribes in the second century BC. The Celts had already destroyed one Roman army, massacred its camp-followers, and now threatened northern Italy. At Aquae Sextiae, the Romans rounded on the barbarians, showing them no mercy. They overran their menfolk and chased the fleeing Celts all the way to their wagon encampment. 'Here the women met them,' wrote Plutarch, 'holding swords and axes in their hands. With hideous shrieks of rage they tried to drive back the hunted and the hunters. The fugitives as deserters, the pursuers as foes. With bare hands the women tore away the shields of the Romans or grasped their swords, enduring mutilating wounds. Their fierce spirit unvanquished to the end.'

A year later, in 101 BC, the Celtic women of the Cimbri were again overwhelmed by the rage of battle. At Vercellae, the victorious Romans were confronted by 'women in black robes who stood at their wagons and slew the fleeing warriors—their husbands, brothers, or fathers—and then strangled their own children and cast them beneath the wheels of their wagons before cutting their own throats.' The savage, desperate pride of the Cimbric women became idealised by Roman historians, who always liked to stress the moral superiority of the barbarians to their own decadent leaders.

Tacitus, in his geography of the German tribes of the first century AD, described occasions when Germanic women encouraged their men in battle by invoking the shame of defeat. 'Armies on the point of collapse', he wrote, 'have been rallied by their women pleading with their men, thrusting forward their bared breasts, and making them realise the imminent prospect of enslavement. A fate which the Germans fear more for their women than themselves.' That this action was not exclusive to the northern barbarians is shown by its occurrence among unmarried women of the Arab Bedouins. To provoke their warriors, they threatened to offer themselves to the enemy, exposing their breasts, unveiling their faces and undoing their braided hair.

It is in the chronicles of Tacitus that we have a portrait of another Celtic queen—Cartimandua. Like Medb, she is a formidable ruler and powerful warlord. She is also a flawed character whose sexuality leads to her downfall. Unlike Medb, she is not a construction of myth, but a true ruler of men living in the middle of the first century AD. When the Romans invaded

Britain for the second time in 43 AD, they intended to stay. In order to protect the prosperous lowlands they conquered in south-east England, they resorted to the strategy that preserved their frontiers elsewhere. By identifying and supporting client rulers among the natives on the fringe of their empire, they ensured a buffer zone between them and the barbarians, at minimum risk and low cost. In northern England, the Roman governor Plautius struck a deal with Cartimandua, leader of the Brigantes, a confederation of tribes whose land stretched both sides of the Pennines across Yorkshire and Lancashire, from the Humber and Mersey to the northern limits of Cumbria. A treaty was made and Cartimandua had her coffers enriched.

Other native rulers of the Britons were not as accommodating as Cartimandua. Caratacus, Celtic king of southern England, stood in the very path of the Roman conquest. There could be no acceptable arrangement for him. He either gave away his territory or fought to the end to defend it. Retreating westwards in 51 AD, he decided on a major confrontation with the Roman army. Recruiting warriors from the Silures in south Wales and the Ordovices in central Wales, he hoped to use the rugged, water-logged Welsh landscape. Caratacus had made a good choice for the time of his rebellion. A new Roman governor had only just arrived in Britain. Publius Ostorius Scapula wasted little time, however, and was fully appraised of the political situation. Although he knew of the treaty with Cartimandua, he also realised the Celtic queen could not possibly maintain control over all her subjects, and there were rumours of a strong anti-Roman faction among the northern tribes. In order to prevent any members of the Brigantes joining with Caratacus in Wales, Scapula began his campaign against the rebel king by advancing into north Wales, cutting off any communication between the two. That his fears were founded on truth was soon revealed when fighting broke out to the rear of his army against warriors from the Brigantes. The insurrection was crushed and its leaders executed, but the rest of the Brigantes were pardoned. This political act suggested that Scapula recognised the friendship of Cartimandua and did not want to punish her people too harshly.

Somewhere in central Wales, along the upper stretches of the River Severn, Caratacus prepared his ground for the battle with Scapula. On a hill overlooking the marshy banks of the river, the Celts constructed an earthen rampart braced with stones and timber. Scapula had an effective force of some 12,000 professional soldiers from the legions XIV *Gemina* and XX *Valeria*, plus several thousand Celtic auxiliaries probably sent by Cartimandua as a sign of good faith. Caratacus rode among his warriors on the day of combat, invoking the spirit of their forefathers who had beaten Julius Caesar back from their shores. Daunted by the physical obstacles before him, Scapula was doubtful of the success of a frontal attack, but his soldiers and officers were keen for battle and demanded an assault. Crossing the river, the Romans immediately came under a hail of spears, arrows and

stones hurled from behind the rampart. Ordering the legionaries to raise their shields above their heads in the famous *testudo*, the Romans pushed on against the rampart, their picks and shovels tugging away at the rocks supporting the wall. With the rampart crumbling beneath them, the will of the Britons broke and they retreated in disorder. The Roman legionaries pursued them in close formation while their auxiliaries hunted any straggling Celts with their javelins. All Caratacus's family was captured, but the king himself escaped. He fled to the realm of Cartimandua.

It seems strange that Caratacus should choose as his place of refuge the court of a leader renowned for her alliance with Rome. This may suggest that Cartimandua's relations with the Romans were not as clear-cut as the history of Tacitus maintains. Already, Scapula had had problems with the Brigantes and maybe the Celtic Queen was waiting to see who triumphed in battle before committing herself to either side. Wherever her sympathies lay, the news of Caratacus's defeat made up her mind. As soon as the beaten

Celtic king arrived on her territory, he was arrested and bound in chains, awaiting the pleasure of the Roman governor. Cartimandua could not afford to align her people with a loser. Her political decision was well rewarded. She received a prize of luxury Roman goods and the assurance that the security of her people would be respected. Her act, considered treacherous by Tacitus and many other historians, had preserved the Celtic sovereignty of northern England. It is incorrect to view her as letting down the cause of British independence as a whole, because Britain at the time was not a united nation but a collection of independent tribes who considered each other just as foreign and dangerous as the Romans.

Over the next five years, Cartimandua continued to rule the Brigantes. Her husband was a nobleman called Venutius, thought by many to have been a ruler in his own right of tribes to the north. That the Brigantes were the more important tribe, and Cartimandua the senior partner, appears true from the fact that Venutius lived in Cartimandua's court and she remained queen of her people. Despite Venutius's likely sympathy for Caratacus, Cartimandua maintained her alliance with the Romans. It is believed she ruled her territory from a hill-fort at Barwick, east of the Pennines near the Ouse valley and the Humber. Between the royal pair, there must have been much cause for antagonism. Their marriage may have been a dynastic decision to strengthen their hold on the north of England, but whereas Venutius hoped it would increase his reputation as the chief male defender of Celtic independence, he must also have envied and resented the personal wealth of Cartimandua, derived from the Romans. If Venutius did come from the relatively poorer tribes to the north of the Brigantes, then there must have been many pillow debates like those between Medb and Ailill, in which each ruler contested the superiority of their wealth and power.

The political strain between Venutius and Cartimandua began to tell and she took her pleasure from her husband's armour-bearer, a young man called Vellocatus. When her husband protested at her flagrant violation of their marriage, she expelled him from her court and raised Vellocatus to be royal consort. Factions in and outside the territory of the Brigantes took sides and Venutius received the support of all those Celtic warlords who wished to reopen the conflict with Rome. Returning to his home base in the north, Venutius did not act fast enough to prevent Cartimandua kidnapping his brother and other members of his family. The Celtic queen hoped this would prevent Venutius from taking any action against her, but the backing of other Celtic chieftains overcame Venutius's concern. He gathered an army of northern tribesmen, many from the Brigantes and even some auxiliaries serving with the Romans. The situation was now serious enough for the Romans to fear for the security of their northern frontier.

At first, Cartimandua called on the Romans to supply a small force to protect her prisoners from Venutius. Didius Gallus was the Roman governor at this time, around 56 AD, and he sent a few cohorts and squadrons of horsemen. Venutius had a powerful army behind him and was far from

Celtic bronze sword scabbard with fittings for a hilt. Found at Cotterdale, north Yorkshire, land of the Brigantes.

dissuaded by the intervention of the Romans. He proceeded to invade the queen's territory and collided with the Roman contingent. The conflict was hard-fought and indecisive. The alarm rang loudly for Gallus and he mobilised *Legio* IX, under the command of Caesius Nasica and based at Longthorpe, near Peterborough. The legion was more successful, its armoured troops eventually defeating the northern Celts. But though the queen was safe, Venutius won control of most of the Brigantian territory. Thereafter, there is no reference to Cartimandua in Tacitus or any other chronicler. From the increased military activity in this region, it appears that Cartimandua never regained control of the majority of northern tribes and the Romans had to rely on building more forts to protect their northern frontier.

Fifteen years later, the Brigantes were conquered by Petillius Cerealis and Yorkshire fell within the Roman Empire. Cartimandua's political balancing act had postponed Roman occupation of northern England longer than other parts of the country, but with her demise there were few Celts able to compromise as successfully as her. Some historians consider Cartimandua to have acted foolishly in her break with Venutius, but it seems clear that the anti-Roman faction among the Brigantes had already won the support of Venutius, so she had no choice but to bring the crisis to a head. That Tacitus should focus upon the queen's affair with Vellocatus as the main cause of the civil war and her downfall—'by that criminal act she lost all authority'—shows that the Roman writer was not too far removed from the male prejudices of the Celtic writers of the *Tain* in their belief that a woman's sexuality flawed her ability to govern.

As the Romans put more and more effort into the conquest of Britain, sending further armies into Wales and northern England, so they desired a greater return on their investment. Roman financiers had loaned vast sums of money to the new colonies and now put pressure on the Romano-British landlords to pay up. In south-east England, Prasutagus, King of the Iceni, died in 60 AD. He left half of his great fortune to his daughters, but willed the other half to the Roman emperor so as to appease the money-grabbing bureaucrats. Unfortunately, the Romans were even more rapacious than the Celts believed. Catus Decianus, chief *procurator*, took it upon himself to absorb the whole of the Celtic king's wealth, no doubt ensuring he retained a goodly proportion for his own retirement. With an army of Roman veterans, too old for active service but brutal enough to ransack a kingdom, he swept over the Icenian teritory and included every field, animal and item of treasure on his inventory. In his way stood Prasutagus's wife, Boudica, and her two daughters. Boudica protested at the sacking of their wealth, but Catus Decianus pillaged her court and had the queen whipped for her impudence. The two royal daughters were cornered by a gang of Roman soldiers and raped.

Dio Cassius describes Boudica as 'very tall, most terrifying in appearance, a fierce eye and harsh voice. A great mass of the tawniest hair fell to her hips. Around her neck she wore a golden torc and over a multi-coloured tunic she wore a thick cloak secured with a brooch.' This description comes 200 years after the event, but without doubt Boudica was a formidable woman. With the insults to her body and her family raging in her mind, she set about preparing a revenge on the Romans that would shock the empire to its core. Tacitus records a series of ill omens presaging that fury. Within the colonial capital of Colchester, the Roman statue of victory toppled from its base, ending up face-down on the ground. Weird sounds unnerved the Romans and some said they saw the image of a city in ruins beneath the River Thames, water that turned red at high tide. A catastrophe was imminent.

Among the Trinovantes, to the south of Colchester, hatred of the Romans was no less intense. Joining with the Iceni of East Anglia, Boudica welcomed them and addressed their chieftains. Dio Cassius imagined her words of counsel. 'You have come to realise now', she said, 'how much better your life was before the Romans. You may have been poorer, but you were free. Wealth with slavery is not worth having. It is our own fault that the Romans are here, for we should have expelled them as we did with Julius Caesar. But even at this late day, let us do our duty while we still remember what freedom is, that we may leave to our children not only its name but also its reality. Have no fear of the Romans, for they need to protect themselves with armour and earthworks, whereas we can fight from the swamps and mountains, eating only the roughest grass and roots. Let us show them they are hares and foxes trying to rule over dogs and wolves.' These Latin words of patriotism are the basis for Boudica's enduring legend as the first great hero of the British nation. It is interesting to note also that the Romans considered the barbarians willing to give up their higher living standards under the empire in pursuit of liberty.

Boudica awaited the best opportunity for revenge. The Governor of Britain, Caius Suetonius Paullinus, had removed the majority of Roman military force to north Wales, where he was endeavouring to break the power of the Druids. South-east England lay open to the Celtic queen. Her main target was the colonial settlement at Colchester. It was from here that many of the semi-retired veterans came to despoil her territory. According to Tacitus, the Romans had neglected the defences of this town in favour of building a temple to the memory of the Emperor Claudius. At the last moment, the Romans desperately called upon Catus Decianus to send them reinforcements, but all he could manage was 200 poorly armed men. Leading an army of several thousand Celtic warriors fired with vengeance, Boudica advanced on Colchester. The Romans were too few to defend the outskirts of the town and withdrew to the half-finished temple. There, they held out for two days until the Celts stormed the walls and slaughtered everyone within—men, women and children. No one escaped Boudica's anger. The settlement was burnt to the ground, leaving only a thin layer of ash for future archaeologists.

Romanised sculpture of the Celtic goddess of the Brigantes holding lance and orb; closest possible imagery to a portrait of Cartimandua. Now in the Royal Museum of Scotland, Edinburgh.

Hearing of the revolt, Paullinus instructed his only available legion, IX *Hispana*, to bring order to the area. Led by Petillius Cerealis, it arrived too late to save Colchester. As they marched through the forest of East Anglia, the victorious Britons followed them, then surrounded and crushed them, isolating the extended line of march and breaking the army into easily eliminated groups. Petillius Cerealis escaped with his life and a few cavalry, but the rest perished. The magnitude of the disaster was enough to make the *procurator*, Catus Decianus, pack his bags, secure his coffers, and sail for the safety of Gaul. Paullinus abandoned his campaign against the island of Anglesey and took command of the crisis himself. If he did not act soon, the whole of Britain would be lost.

Sailing to Chester and then riding 180 miles (300 km) to London, Paullinus could have arrived ahead of his main body of troops within four days. London was not as large as the Roman colony at Colchester, but it was an important trading post inhabited by wealthy merchants. The town was seized by panic. The richest merchants had already fled in their boats to join Catus Decianus in Gaul. The remaining citizens pleaded with Paullinus to defend them against Boudica, but the Roman governor was a soldier at heart and could see it was no position to defend. He made the decision to abandon the settlement and recommended the merchants to retreat south-wards into Kent, where the Celtic ruler was still loyal to the Romans. Riding back along Watling Street, he rejoined the majority of his army methodically marching through the Midlands.

By the time Boudica rode her chariot towards London, most of its inhabitants had gone, leaving only the poor and the sick. With no opposition, the Britons easily stormed the town and slaughtered the people in an orgy of atrocity. Soon after, the Celtic horde swept over the settlement of St Albans, slaying the Romanised Britons there as collaborators. Tacitus writes that the Britons were not interested in preserving prisoners and subsequently 70,000 Roman citizens perished. The actual figure was probably much smaller than this as the majority of people would have evacuated the war zone, but the Romans were outraged by rumours of Celtic torture and mutilation and prepared themselves for a confrontation with the warrior queen.

Paullinus numbered among his soldiers the whole of the *legio* XIV *Gemina*, plus a detachment of veterans from *legio* XX *Valeria* and auxiliaries from forts he passed on the way, a total of around 10,000 men. He also requested the support of *legio* II *Augusta*, but its commander, Poenius Postumus, at Exeter refused to spare his men, perhaps feeling his own position was in danger. He later committed suicide by falling on his sword. It seems likely that Paullinus met up with his army at Wall, near Lichfield, and from here planned his move against Boudica. As the Britons marched onwards from St Albans along Watling Street towards the north west, Paullinus chose his ground carefully. He positioned his men with an open plain before them and a thick wood protecting their flanks and back. His

Roman helmet of the first century AD. Cartimandua's Celtic warriors adopted many Roman weapons when they campaigned together. From the State Prehistorical Collection, Munich.

legionary foot-soldiers assembled in the centre of the battle formation, while the cavalry formed on the wings and the lightly armed auxiliaries were either stationed in reserve or moved around the battleground in loose packs, seeking opportunities.

Boudica arrived on the battlefield at the head of a vast, exhilarated horde of warriors, escaped slaves and Celtic bandits—all drawn together by the prospect of overthrowing Roman tyranny and sacking the imperial coffers. With them travelled their wives and families, in wagons assembled at the rear in a manner similar to that of the Cimbri and Teutones. If necessary, the wagons made a mobile fortress to which they could retreat. Before her ranks of warriors—some on horseback, some on foot; all carrying large shields, long spears and swords—Boudica rode in her chariot, exhorting them to a famous victory. Tacitus imagined her speech.

'This is not the first time the Britons have been led to battle by a woman,' she proclaimed. 'But I do not take to arms merely to boast of an ancient

89

lineage or even to regain my kingdom and possessions. I fight, like the humblest warrior among you, to assert my liberty and seek revenge for the physical outrages wrought on myself and my daughters. For the proud, arrogant Romans hold nothing sacred. Everyone is victim to their violation. Old women like me endure the scourge and virgins are raped. Look around and view your numbers. Behold the proud display and consider the motives for drawing your sword. On this ground we must either conquer or die with glory. There is no alternative. Although a woman, my decision is made. The men, if they wish, may survive in shame and live in bondage.'

In classic Roman style, Tacitus has Paullinus reply with an equally dramatic speech. 'Ignore the savage roar of these undisciplined barbarians,' he commanded. 'There are more women than men in the horde before you. And the men have no armour and no resolve, so they will break before your ranks, become the refuse of your swords. Remember—keep your order, hurl your javelins, rush forward to close attack, knock them down with your shields and cut a path with your swords. Pursue the vanquished, but never think of plunder. Victory will bring you everything.' To these military instructions, Dio Cassius added a few statements of imperial racial supremacy. 'Above all, victory will be ours: first, because the gods are our allies; second, because of the courage that is our heritage, since we are Romans and have triumphed over all mankind; third, because of our experience; and fourth, because of our prestige, for those we are about to fight are our slaves whom we conquered even when they were free.'

The Celts began the battle. Boudica rolled forward in her chariot, brandishing a spear. Her warriors rushed wildly against the Roman formations, yelling and screaming, hoping to break the nerve of the Romans with the ferocity of their appearance. Used to the Celtic manner of warfare, the Romans held their ground, knowing the tribesmen would exhaust themselves in the first onslaught. As the two sides closed, a storm of javelins, spears and stones clattered on each other's shields. With the sharply barked orders of their centurions, the Romans then pressed forward, using their shields as Paullinus had instructed, breaking through the Celtic lines in a wedge formation. The auxiliaries followed them through, while the cavalry closed in on the Celtic flanks, crowding the wounded and dying tribesmen together.

Dio Cassius describes a haphazard combat in which the Romans broke into groups surrounded by the greater number of Celts. Auxiliaries hurled javelins at their lightly armoured opponents. Roman archers tackled the British chariots. The legionaries exchanged sword blows with the more heavily armoured tribesmen. This continued late into the day, until the Romans eventually prevailed. Seeing no way forward among the piles of bodies, the Britons at the rear forgot the proud commands of their leader and ran.

Pressing on over the mangled bodies, the Romans pursued the Celts to their wagons and fought with their women, just as they had at Aquae

Roman soldiers raiding a barbarian village. Drawing from the Column of Antoninus, Rome.

Sextiae. Intoxicated with the adrenalin of victory, the Romans spared neither men, women, nor cattle. No less than 80,000 Britons died, wrote Tacitus. The triumph was decisive. Enough Celts had fallen that day for the rebellion to end almost immediately. Stricken by the failure of defeat, Boudica could see no way out but to end her life. According to Tacitus, she took poison. In Dio Cassius, Boudica fell ill and died. Whatever the truth, she did not survive her warriors.

The rebellion of Boudica profoundly shook the empire-makers at Rome. The Emperor Nero ordered an inquiry immediately and sent a special envoy to deal with the Britons and establish an enduring peace. Paullinus was not a politician and preferred the devastation of the warrior. Receiving

reinforcements from Germany, he punished the Britons by wasting their land and bringing on a famine. The new *procurator*, Julius Classicianus, a replacement for Catus Decianus, was horrified at the unforgiving attitude of Paullinus. He urged Rome to recall Paullinus, knowing peace could not be established while the warlord remained in Britain. Eventually, a policy of reconciliation was adopted and Paullinus recalled. It is a tribute to Boudica and the ferocity of her revolt that even the powerful men in Rome had to realise that the Britons could never be silenced by force and that they should implement a more civilised policy of peaceful coexistence.

Boadicea and her Daughters, a bronze statue on the Victoria Embankment, London, designed by Thomas Thornycroft in 1856, but unveiled in 1902. It represents the Victorian vision of Boudica as a fighter for British liberty against tyranny—more a Britannia than a Briton.

Women of Christ

**AETHELFLAED,
MATILDA
OF TUSCANY,
ELEANOR OF
AQUITAINE**

The *Annals of Ulster* say nothing of the deaths of Alfred the Great and his successful son Edward. They were not important. The *Annals* save their praise for Aethelflaed of Mercia—'*famosissima regina Saxonum*'—celebrated Queen of the Saxons, conqueror of the Vikings. Her death was a major loss to the cause of Saxon and Celt alike who fought to rid their land of the pagan invaders. And yet, her fame has been lost over the centuries, diminished by the reputation of her male contemporaries. The reason for this is not sexual prejudice, but political design. The Anglo-Saxon chroniclers wrote their history for the West Saxon court, to create a history of their land in which the old Saxon kingdom of Mercia accepted the rule of Wessex and became absorbed in the emerging united nation of England. They could not afford to build up the reputation of a Mercian ruler. No matter how significant her contribution, it would endanger the seniority of Wessex. It is a measure of Aethelflaed's political intelligence that she played her role in the rise of England under the West Saxons and sacrificed her own Mercian identity to provide a united front against the Vikings.

Aethelflaed began her political career as a diplomatic gift. The eldest daughter of Alfred the Great, she was presented in her late teens to Aethelred, Ealdorman of Mercia. Alfred believed the only way the Saxons could defeat the Vikings, living in eastern and northern England, was to bring the various royal families of the Saxons together in alliance. This was sealed by intermarriage. The kingdom of Wessex covered land in southern England. Mercia lay to the north of it in the western Midlands, from the Welsh border to the Danish border of East Anglia. Already, Aethelred had accepted the authority of Alfred and the West Saxons by refusing to claim the kingship of Mercia, preferring to call himself Ealdorman. He was absolute ruler of Mercia, but above all he was a loyal and responsible ally of Alfred. It was within this atmosphere of necessary political friendship that Aethelflaed first learnt the facts of life about England's survival against the rapacious Vikings. When Alfred died in 899, Aethelred remained steady and reaffirmed his support to Alfred's son, Edward, brother of his wife

Aethelflaed. Aethelred was many years older than his wife and, in the last few years of his reign, Aethelflaed began to assert herself and take command of Mercian affairs, but always in conjunction with her brother Edward. Together, they would hold the ground Alfred had won and in time they would throw the Vikings out of their territory.

In 911, Aethelred died. Aethelflaed was probably around 40 and well established among the Mercian nobility. By birth she was half-Mercian—her mother was Ealhswith, daughter of a Mercian Ealdorman—and her aristocratic supporters had themselves been brought up in the spirit of political accord. Little contemporary record has survived of Aethelflaed's private life or her personality. There is, however, a reference to her in the twelfth-century history of William of Malmesbury, who describes her as 'a powerful member of king Edward's party, the delight of her subjects, and the dread of his enemies.' He goes on to explain that, following the painful birth of her first child, she refused to sleep with her husband, saying it was 'unbecoming the daughter of a king to give way to a delight which after a time produced such painful consequences.' The story seems influenced by Amazon associations that surrounded any woman warlord, a similar tale being told of Zenobia. Despite this cliché, William of Malmesbury is determined to emphasise her contribution to her brother's government. 'This spirited heroine assisted her brother greatly with her advice,' he wrote, 'was of equal service in building cities, and, whether through fortune or her own efforts, was a woman who protected men at home and intimidated them abroad.'

In keeping with her husband's wishes and to maintain the political alliance with her brother, Aethelflaed refused the title of queen and continued her husband's tradition, calling herself *Myrcna hlaefdige* (Lady of the Mercians) the exact equivalent of Aethelred's *Myrcna hlaford*. This official title was acceptable to Edward and Wessex, but outside the Saxon kingdoms she won sufficient respect from neighbouring powers to be called queen. As Aethelflaed and Edward mourned the passing of a mighty warrior and faithful ally of their father, they began to conceive a new strategy. Edward was probably the dominant figure in the relationship and after Aethelred's death, he seized London, Oxford and the southern territories of Mercia. His ultimate intention was clear, but he was politic enough not to push the Mercians too far. In the previous year, the Northumbrians had broken their truce with Edward and raided Mercia. Edward wielded sufficient authority in his sister's territory to send forth Mercians as well as West Saxons against the invaders. In the same year, taking on her husband's responsibility of defence, Aethelflaed complemented the mobile units of her brother by building a fortress at Bremesburh.

In the year following Aethelred's death, Aethelflaed oversaw the building of two more fortresses, at Scergeat and Bridgnorth. In 913, fortifications rose at Tamworth and Stafford; in 914 at Eddisbury and Warwick; and in 915 at Chirbury, Weardburh and Runcorn. This was to be

Woman warlord from a
Romanesque (probably
twelfth century) manuscript
representing the vice of
superbia-pride from
Prudentius's *Psychomachia*.

the backbone of the Saxon strategy against the Vikings. Edward matched
her sister's building with forts in the south, at Hertford, Witham,
Buckingham, Bedford and Maldon, all over the same four years. The plan
was to use these forts as bases both for defence and offence. If the Vikings
raided deep into Mercia, then they might ignore the fortifications completely, but when they returned along the strategic routes dominated by the
forts, they were vulnerable to Saxon counter-attacks. Similarly, the forts

could be used as bases to gather troops and supplies before launching a campaign into Viking territory. But a major offensive was not to be entered into too quickly. Edward and Aethelflaed wished to consolidate the hold on their territory.

The forts Aethelflaed established across the north Midlands were not so much military strongholds as fortified settlements, called burhs. They were new towns specifically designed to exploit the economic benefits of an area, as well as serve its strategic purposes. When no natural defences were available, the burhs were laid out in Roman fashion with rectangular earth ramparts. The ramparts were reinforced with timber and stone, sharply scarped at the front, gently sloping at the rear. Some may have been 10 feet (3 m) high and 20 feet (6 m) wide, with an extra, smaller stone wall behind them. At Tamworth in Staffordshire, the rampart was doubled in width near the gateway and probably had a bridge over the gate to ensure a continuous walkway. Beyond the ramparts were several ditches. Inside, the streets were planned as a gridiron, with easy access to a ring road running along the wall. Several forts were set on important routes within Mercia, such as Chirbury, within 2 miles (3 km) of Offa's Dyke, overseeing the road through Montgomery into central Wales. Stafford, Tamworth, Warwick and Buckingham formed a diagonal front line with Danish north-eastern England. These forts were sited directly opposite the Danish military centres at Derby, Leicester and Northampton, each within 30 miles (48 km) of its enemy. Aethelflaed's line of forts joined up with those in southern England and it seems very clear that the building campaign was a co-ordinated act between her and Edward.

The Danish Vikings of eastern England were not Aethelflaed's only enemies. In north-west England, considerable inroads were being made by Irish and Norwegian settlers. Some settled around the Mersey in Wirral and led damaging raids against Chester. To combat this and the generally unstable situation in Northumbria, she built the forts of Runcorn and Eddisbury to add to the fortifications at Chester. The Welsh were not friendly either, and several of Aethelflaed's forts in western Mercia, such as Chirbury, may also have acted as front-line forts when Viking animosity relaxed and Saxon fought Briton. In 916, she was compelled to send an army into Wales to storm Brecenanmere at Llangorse lake, near Brecon. There, she captured a Welsh king's wife and 33 members of his court. The campaign was such a success that the Welsh kings submitted to her authority. In the following year, Viking war-bands from Northampton and Leicester led a major raid against southern Mercia. The Danish horsemen ravaged several towns and slaughtered their inhabitants. The time had come for Aethelflaed and Edward to lead a co-ordinated counter-attack into Viking territory.

In the summer of 917, Edward ordered a two-pronged assault. In the south, the Danes had attempted to besiege his forts, but given up. In retaliation, he stormed their fortifications at Colchester and Tempsford and

Viking warriors wearing boar-crested helmets similar to that discovered at Benty Grange in Derbyshire. Drawing from a bronze matrix for making repoussé panels to decorate helmets, found at Torslunda, Oland, Sweden.

slew a Danish king and his son. The Danes of East Anglia then recruited mercenary pirates for an assault on Maldon. Again, they lacked the staying-power to carry a siege and were chased away by the garrison. Edward followed up by moving further into Danish territory and forcing the submission of the Vikings at Northampton and Huntingdon. In East Anglia and Essex, the Danish army swore their allegiance to Edward, saying 'they wished all that he wished, protecting all that he protected, by sea and land.'

While Edward triumphed in the south, Aethelflaed led an army against Derby. It has been suggested that the Viking army of Derby was absent at the time, fighting in the south against Edward. If this is true, then it shows the good strategic sense of Aethelflaed. Exploiting the diversion wrought by her brother, Aethelflaed took the Viking military centre without need of a siege. But her entry into Derby was not completely unopposed. Four of her closest thanes were cut down within the gates of the town. By the winter of 917, the Viking armies of East Anglia, Cambridge, Bedford, Huntingdon, Northampton and Derby had ceased to exist or offered their allegiance to Edward. Brother and sister planned the next step.

In spring 918, Edward advanced on Stamford. At the same time, Aethelflaed led her troops against Leicester. Once more, the garrison at Leicester may have been diverted by Edward's movements or perhaps they were simply overawed by Aethelflaed's army. Whatever the reason, the lady of the Mercians secured the key fortress by peaceful means and received the submission of the Danish forces stationed there. Such was the fear engendered by the rolling triumph of the Saxon war-machine that the Viking citizens of York, a long way to the north of Leicester, also sent their pledges of submission and loyalty. Only two major Viking strongholds, at Nottingham and Lincoln, remained. But at the height of her power, in June 918, at Tamworth, Aethelflaed fell ill and died. It must have been a cruel blow to her brother Edward, both emotionally and militarily. Together they had masterminded the campaign and yet she would not be there to conclude it. Aethelflaed was buried in the monastery of St Peter's at Gloucester.

After her funeral, Edward wasted no time in assuming control of Aethelflaed's army at Tamworth. All the noblemen of Mercia recognised Edward's superior strength and made their submission to him. There would be no succession crisis, even though many Mercians resented their loss of nationality. The reality of Wessex as the dominant power in England was upon them. Even the kings of Wales recognised his authority, though this was more an acknowledgement of Aethelflaed's power than his own. With the full support of Mercia, Edward got back in his saddle and seized the remaining Viking strongholds in the Midlands. All settlements south of the Humber were back under English control after 40 years of Danish rule. Edward was undoubtedly the master of this remarkable triumph, but the chronicles of his court have depreciated the crucial role of his sister. Without her firm support and faith in the cause of Wessex, without her own considerable military and political ability, Edward would not have been able to fulfil his brilliant strategy. Together, Aethelflaed and Edward devised and executed a remarkable victory, one that set the stage for a united England free of Viking dominance. But because of the propaganda demands that Edward be seen as the chief author of the victory, and Aethelflaed's acquiescence in her subsidiary role, her full contribution has been lost. It was only in foreign courts that chroniclers could be free in their praise of Aethelflaed as the most famous queen of the Saxons.

In Italy in the eleventh century, there was no such problem for Matilda, Countess of Tuscany. Her fame grew throughout the Middle Ages until, in the seventeenth century, her remains were removed to Rome and reinterred in St Peter's with a splendid marble effigy by Bernini, holding the papal crown and the keys of St Peter. In such high regard was she held by succeeding popes that it is surprising she was never canonised. Certainly, many of the Catholic histories written about her at the end of the nineteenth century are virtual hagiographies. In Italy, she is simply called *La Gran Contessa*. The secret of her fame lay in her tenacious defence of the Italian papacy against the German emperor, one of the chief struggles dominating southern Europe in the Middle Ages.

Matilda's father, Boniface of Canossa, was assassinated in 1052 when she was only six. It has been said he was the victim of a plot hatched by the Emperor Henry III. A little later, Matilda's brother and sister died, leaving

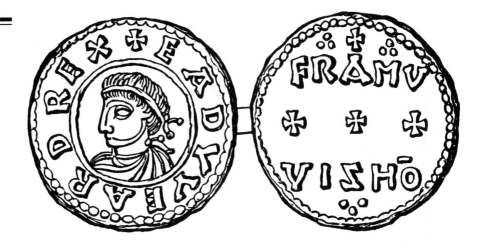

Coin of Edward the Elder, King of England, son of Alfred and brother of Aethelflaed.

her the sole heir to the House of Canossa. It was a vast land-holding, including the whole of Tuscany, parts of Liguria and Umbria and the cities of Ferrara, Verona, Mantua, Reggio, Parma, Lucca, Pisa, Florence, Pistoia, Modena, Spoleto and Camerino. The greatest concentration of power in the Italian peninsula, it was a prime target for German emperors always seeking estates south of the Alps. Her mother, Beatrice, knew Matilda would have to fight to preserve her inheritance. Alongside the usual courtly education of a lady, Matilda learned to ride and handle sword and lance. 'Disdaining with a virile spirit the art of Arachne, she seized the spear of Pallas,' wrote the seventeenth-century historian Vedriani. He also claims that two suits of armour worn by her were sold in 1622 *a vil prezzo* at the market-place in Reggio. Above all, the young woman spent time studying the defences of her castle at Canossa, the formidable family seat. Situated on a massive outcrop of rock some 1,500 feet (450 m) up in the Apennines outside Reggio, it dominated the landscape for miles.

The suspicious death of her father and the vulnerability of her estates led Matilda's mother to marry Godfrey, Duke of Upper Lorraine. He was a powerful enemy of Henry III and in retaliation the German emperor temporarily held Beatrice hostage. This ill-treatment further deepened Matilda's animosity to his empire. In 1059, at the age of 15, Matilda left her home on the rock of Canossa and rode with her mother and stepfather to Rome. The spectacle of the papacy and her family's good relations with the Pope greatly impressed the young woman. Ever after, her animosity towards the emperor burgeoned into a passionate loyalty to the papacy. Her first opportunity to demonstrate this allegiance occurred two years later. A new Pope had been elected, but he was not favoured by the mother of the new, young Emperor Henry IV. She put forward her own candidate, Cadalous, Bishop of Parma, and recruited an army of knights and levies. The papacy called upon the Normans in southern Italy to assist, but they were engaged in fighting for their own domains, leaving Beatrice and Godfrey to raise their own troops from the knights and peasants of Tuscany. Matilda

99

led a small vanguard against Cadalous as he crossed the northern border of Tuscany. The fighting was inconclusive and the antipope continued towards Rome.

With the late addition of an army of mercenaries raised by the Pope, Godfrey was compelled to hold his defence of Rome until the imperial forces were actually within the city. Fighting broke out in the Trasteverine quarter and around the Castel St Angelo held by Romans supporting Cadalous. In the conflict, Matilda shared with Arduino della Palude the command of 400 archers, the same number of warriors armed with pikes, and a detachment of horsemen. In a bid to rejoin her stepfather's forces, Matilda led a fiercesome charge against the schismatics, forcing the part led by Guibert of Ravenna to retreat back to their entrenchments on the fields of Nero outside the city. In victory, Matilda was reputed to be magnanimous and she ordered her troops to spare the lives of the imperialist prisoners, punishing only those freebooters who had ravaged the Roman suburbs. With little hope of pursuing his cause, Cadalous returned to Parma. Godfrey, Beatrice and their daughter Matilda had struck their first military blow against the empire.

In 1069, Matilda strengthened her association with the anti-imperialist cause by marrying Godfrey's son and heir, known as Godfrey the Hunchback. For a short time, she lived in Lorraine and gave birth to a child. But the child died in infancy and Matilda returned to Italy. Godfrey was not made of the same fibre as his father and the dynastic marriage faltered. He did not support the papacy as actively as Matilda wished and the two separated. Godfrey attempted a reconciliation, but rumour bound his name with an assassination attempt on the Pope and Matilda vowed never to see him again. Two years later, in 1076, Godfrey was murdered. In the same year, Beatrice died in Pisa. Her passing was mourned greatly by the papacy and most of all by Matilda. All those who had guided Matilda through the troubled times of the past two decades were dead. Alone, she would have to make decisions determining the fate of herself and her lands. Various rulers across Europe offered their proposal of marriage to the powerful widow, among them Robert, eldest son of William the Conqueror, and the Emperor of Constantinople. But for support and advice, Matilda turned to Pope Gregory VII.

In the same year, Henry IV took charge of imperial affairs in Germany and exerted his authority over Church lands in Italy. When this was criticised by the papacy, he accused the Pope of licentiousness and necromancy, calling upon the clergy to depose him. In response, Gregory VII sent him notice of excommunication. Henry had badly misjudged his attack on the papacy for the excommunication gave his enemies in Germany reason to rise against him. The young emperor was in real danger of losing his throne. In a desperate attempt to backtrack, Henry crossed the Alps to ask the Pope's forgiveness. Under an armed escort provided by Matilda, Gregory rode through Tuscany to meet the emperor. Matilda was fearful

that Henry might use this occasion to ambush the Pope. She recommended he stay with her at the castle of Canossa: no army could take that stronghold. And so it was that in January 1077, the German emperor ascended the steep snowy slopes to Canossa and made a formal submission to Gregory VII. It was staged cruelly to exact the most humiliation out of Henry's plight. Alone, and without his royal robes, clad only in a woollen shirt and with bare feet, he was kept waiting outside the Pope's quarters for three days. Only after this abasement was Henry allowed into Gregory's presence, where he lay face down on the ground and begged forgiveness. Gregory declared the emperor's penance was at an end.

The depth of Henry's submission does not seem to have bothered the emperor, although it disgusted many of his supporters. Just three years later, he felt secure enough to defy Gregory and elect an antipope. Again, Gregory excommunicated him, but this time the clergy of northern Italy were eager to break away from the Pope's rule and sided with the schismatics. At the Battle of Volta, on Mantuan territory, Matilda's troops were defeated by the imperialists and forced to flee. Town after town rebelled against her authority. Matilda retreated to Canossa to sit out the storm, but the situation grew worse. In 1081, Henry invaded Italy and made directly for Rome. The siege was ineffectual and the emperor returned to Lucca, one of Matilda's former vassals. From there, he thoroughly ravaged her territory. So hard pressed was she that she was unable to send her usual contingents of troops to defend the Pope. Instead, she melted down part of her treasure and sent that to Gregory. More and more of her supporters turned to the emperor and joined him in another assault on Rome. Every summer, however, the intense heat forced the majority of Henry's soldiers to retreat north to Tuscany and pillage again Matilda's territory. By 1084, Henry was in command of most of Rome, the Pope and his supporters only holding out in the Castel St Angelo. Considering victory was his, Henry had himself and his wife crowned by their antipope in St Peter's.

With Matilda fighting for her own survival in Tuscany, Gregory turned to Robert Guiscard and his Norman warriors in the south. Several times, his messengers failed to prevail upon the Norman warlord, but eventually, hearing of Henry's antics in Rome and fearing an unfriendly power to his north, Guiscard turned his attention to Rome. The word of his advance struck terror in the emperor. Claiming he had important business to attend in Germany, Henry fled the city with the antipope in his baggage train. The Normans were renowned throughout Europe and Henry did not wish to test their prowess. Riding with the Normans were many Muslim mercenaries.

Their reputation not only frightened Henry but concerned the Romans so much that they took a stand against Guiscard and tried to prevent his army entering the city. Their defence angered the Normans and their Saracen allies swept through the city, wreaking the most terrible outrages on the citizens. The soldiery were beyond Guiscard's control and only after Gregory's impassioned plea did the Norman warlord curb the destruction.

The safety of Gregory raised the morale of Matilda and her supporters. As Henry retreated through Tuscany, she received news that the schismatic Bishops of Reggio and Parma had halted before Sorbara, one of her castles in Modena. Proceeding from Canossa, she led a small force of horsemen and foot-soldiers. Coming close to the enemy line, Matilda waited until nightfall before sending her troops against them. Breaking the silence with cries of St Peter, the Tuscan men-at-arms plunged among the tents of the imperialists. 'The soldiers of the enemy were buried in sleep,' wrote the eighteenth-century historian Fiorentini, 'when suddenly they were struck in the ears by the formidable sound of the name of the Apostolic Vicar of Christ and at the same moment in the vitals by the sword, and thus they passed from the lethergy of sleep to the velocity of death.' The surprise assault was a great success and Matilda captured the Bishops of Parma and Reggio, six commanding noblemen, 100 knights, and 500 horses. This would have been among the last good news Gregory received, for by the end of the year the exhausted Pope was dead and again Matilda was left without a loyal friend.

Despite Henry's swift retreat from Italy, his campaign had been far from a failure and he maintained both political and military pressure on the papacy. He particularly kept a close eye on Matilda, for whatever decision she made about the future of her possessions greatly affected him. In 1089 Matilda finally agreed upon a second union of dynastic advantage. This time, at the age of 43, she married the 17-year-old Welf V, Duke of Bavaria and Carinthia, Marquis of the Marches of Verona, and a member of the Este family. It is likely that the marriage was recommended by the new Pope, Urban II, who wanted to see a friendly state stretching from Tuscany to Bavaria, between him and the emperor. Such was the anger of Henry on hearing of this alliance that he embarked on a second major invasion of Italy.

Mantua and Ferrara fell to the emperor, preferring to open their gates rather than endure an assault. He then advanced to Montebello, where the citizens took a stronger line and refused his bribes. Tiring of the siege, Henry built a massive war-engine to storm the walls. Matilda sent a company of raiders into the area and burnt the machine. Henry called off the siege but resolved to attack Canossa, the scene of his humiliation a decade before. Arriving at Caviliano, now called San Polo d'Enza, he made camp near the little village on the River Enza. Matilda divided her considerable forces and sent half to Bianello, a fortress standing close to three other small castles commanding the mountainous entrance to one of the roads to Canossa. Unaware of this manoeuvre, Henry moved his army

Anglo-Saxon brass inlaid stirrups, tenth century. Stirrups were first worn in England in this century, though their introduction was probably only gradual, as good horsemanship did not depend on them.

closer to the main castle on the rock. He ordered his men to close all routes to the castle and prepare for a lengthy siege. He was determined to finish the reign of Matilda.

Matilda provided her castle with enough provisions to withstand a siege, but she knew it was not good for morale or the support of her vassals throughout Tuscany to be held too long by Henry's army. She chose attack as the best strategy and ordered her finest men-at-arms to prepare for action. Donning a coat of mail, her squires brought her a helmet with nasal and a kite-shaped shield. Early one autumnal morning, she quietly led her warriors out of a secret entrance at the base of the walls of Canossa and descended among the rocks towards the imperialist camp. A dense fog had risen from the Tuscan landscape and shrouded Matilda's movements, only the clinking of spurs and blades indicated their presence. Slitting the throats of weary guards, Matilda's soldiers burst upon the camp, shouting their war-cry of St Peter, encouraged by a chorus of psalms sung by monks from the turrets of her castle. Henry called an immediate retreat, but the panicked imperialists fell back in a rout and were cut to pieces by Matilda's warriors stationed at Bianello. The emperor escaped the slaughter, but his standard was captured and paraded among Matilda's supporters. It was the end of Henry's ambitions in Italy and the beginning of his troubles at home.

The north Italian cities now had enough confidence to acknowledge their independence from imperial influence. Matilda led a league of Lombard cities, including Milan and Cremona, in a 20-year union against Henry. In return, she was granted control of the Alpine passes to prevent any future invasions. She was the strong woman of northern Italy and began to exert her will on Henry's territory, encouraging his son Conrad to rebel against him. In 1106, Henry died, worn out by failure. Matilda could not hide her pleasure—'giving thanks to God who had at last given peace to the Church.' In her final years, Matilda became an object of veneration and even Henry V, the new emperor, was keen to visit her when he arrived in Italy in 1110 for his coronation. His arrival was more of an invasion, however, and it is an indication of Matilda's growing world-weariness that she did little to prevent his vandalism. There would be no more great battles against the German invaders. That would be left to future warlords, male or female. In 1115, Matilda was dead. Buried at San Benedetto near Mantua, her body lay there for 500 years until the Papacy felt in need of her spiritual support during the religious crises of the seventeenth century.

Matilda was one of the greatest landowners of the High Middle Ages. In later centuries, the Salic Law was reinforced in France to prevent a woman becoming sovereign and this affected the rights of inheritance of noble-women further down the social scale. Before this crisis in the fourteenth century, Germanic feudal law was more flexible and not only a daughter, but a wife, could find herself at the head of a fief on her husband's death. This encouraged many noblewomen to take a more active interest in the affairs of their estates. In the late eleventh century, Countess Helwise feared

Matilda, Countess of Tuscany, portrayed with a man-at-arms and a monk, probably her biographer Donizo. From Donizo's twelfth-century *Vita Mathildis*, now in the Vatican Library, Rome.

M ATHILDIS LUCENS: PRECOR HOCCAPE CARAVOLUMEN:

for the security of her land in Evreux, north-west France, and urged her husband, William, Count of Evreux, to war. Orderic Vitalis, in his chronicle of the combat, is highly contemptuous of the woman's role. 'Countess Helwise took offence at insults uttered by Isabel of Conches,' he wrote, 'and used all her influence with Count William and his barons to take up arms. Thus, through the quarrelling of women, the hearts of brave men were stirred to rage and there was much bloodshed, the burning of farms and villages.'

Orderic goes on to describe their characters. 'Both ladies dominated their husbands and oppressed their vassals, terrorising them in various ways. But they were also very different. Helwise was clever and eloquent, but cruel and grasping. Whereas Isabel was generous, bold and bright. When her vassals took to war, she rode armed as a knight, showing no less courage among her men-at-arms than did Camilla, heroine of Italy among the soldiers of Turnus. Nor was she inferior to Lampeto and Marpesia. Hippolyte and Penthesileia, and the other warrior queens of the Amazons who ruled the kings of Asia and are described by Pompeius Trogus and Virgil.' No medieval historian could resist any demonstration of his classical knowledge.

The feud between Helwise, Isabel and their husbands raged on throughout 1091. The actual reason for the conflict appears to lie in the disputed granting of territory in Normandy following the Norman conquest of Britain. Count William fought against his brother, Ralph of Tosny, husband of Isabel. The fighting took the form of raid and counter-raid, with the ordinary people of northern France suffering most. Ralph brought in the assistance of the King of England and after three years, the war came to an end. Helwise had a strong character and continued to dominate her husband's affairs. Around 1108, the elderly count was content to concentrate on the foundation of a monastery, leaving his wife to govern the estate. 'Distinguished by her wit and beauty,' writes Orderic, 'she was one of the tallest women in Evreux. She was the daughter of William, Count of Nevers.'

Preferring to follow her own opinions, Helwise ignored the advice of her husband's barons. She was ambitious to expand her husband's territory and outraged the sensibilities of neighbouring Norman landlords. They denounced her to the King of France and she pushed his tolerance too far by destroying one of his castles in Evreux. The king rounded on Helwise, deprived her and her husband of their property in Normandy and forced them into exile in Anjou. In 1114, the countess died, followed shortly after by her husband. As they died without issue, their territory was annexed by the king.

Eleanor of Aquitaine was a landowner on a magnificent scale. In 1137, at the age of 15, on her father's death and with no brother to usurp her right, she inherited a vast estate stretching from the River Loire to the Pyrenees, including the Duchies of Aquitaine and Gascony and the county of Poitou.

Ruins of the castle at Canossa in the Tuscan Apennines, the formidable stronghold of Matilda's government.

The land was greater than that held by the King of France. And because of this, Eleanor could not be allowed to dispose of the estate as her emotions or mind dictated. The Capetian dynasty closed in on the young woman and made her Queen of France, thus more than doubling the land held by Louis VII. Overwhelmed by her sudden elevation from privileged teenager to Queen of France, Eleanor enjoyed the role of dutiful consort. By her middle twenties, her character demanded more challenging involvement in the politics of the day. When, in 1146, Louis took the cross, Eleanor joined him and together, in the following year, they travelled to the Holy Land. It was not unusual for noble wives to ride with their husbands on crusade. The journey took many years and was regarded as a Grand Tour. Louis probably also felt that such a valuable and headstrong wife as Eleanor should not be left alone in Paris.

The presence of Eleanor with her noblewomen friends, plus wagons of female servants, did not go without criticism from male chroniclers who liked to make punning remarks on the after-dark relations between soldiers and maids—*castra non casta*: there was nothing chaste about their encampments. In order to demonstrate her active role in the campaign or just out of sheer fun, Eleanor insisted on dressing herself and her ladies-in-waiting in full knightly armour. A Greek chronicler, Niketas Choniates,

107

describes their entry into Constantinople. 'I speak of the campaign of the Germans, joined by other kindred nations,' he wrote. 'Females were numbered among them, riding horseback in the manner of men, not on coverlets sidesaddle, but unashamedly astride, bearing lances and weapons as men do. Dressed in masculine garb, they conveyed a wholly martial appearance, more mannish than the Amazons. One stood out from the rest as another Penthesileia and from the embroidered gold which ran around the hem and fringes of her garments was called Goldfoot.' She was Eleanor.

That this may have been more martial chic than active involvement is revealed in the first combat of Eleanor's crusade. As they rode through Asia Minor, Louis took command of the rear while various barons took turns to press ahead with the vanguard. One of the leading knights was Geoffrey of Rancon, a favourite of Eleanor and her vassal. Along the gorges of Pisidia, near Mount Cadmos, Geoffrey took his warriors further ahead than he should, losing touch with the main body of warriors who had spread themselves thinly to guard the long baggage train. It was the moment the Turks had been waiting for. Gangs of bandits swooped down from the mountains and showered the wagons with arrows. Louis took personal command of their defence and fought bravely, killing many Turks. Eleanor, at this point out of sight of any impressionable chroniclers and probably riding in a wagon with her servants, took no part in the action at all. The next day, Geoffrey returned to the main part of the expedition, seeing lines of corpses awaiting burial. The fault of the ambush was placed squarely on his shoulders and he was compelled to return to France or be strung up there and then. His failure reflected on Eleanor and thereafter her presence on the crusade drew only further criticism.

In Antioch, the crusaders paused to consider their next step. While Louis considered plans to reach Jerusalem, Eleanor renewed her friendship with Raymond, prince of the city and her uncle. Only a few years older than her, he was a handsome and effective knight. All the chroniclers suggest some romantic attachment between them. Raymond presumed the French crusaders would help him recapture Edessa, a sound strategic objective that would protect the Western presence in the Holy Land. Louis, however, was insistent on his vow to reach Jerusalem. Eleanor sided with Raymond's reasoning and refused to carry on with her husband. Louis invoked his marital rights, insisting she ride with him. To this, Eleanor brought the full force of her fury. She announced their marriage was not valid in the eyes of God, for they were related through various family connections to an extent prohibited by Church law. This hurt Louis deeply, above all else, he was a strongly pious man.

William of Tyre in his twelfth-century chronicle reflects French suspicion of Raymond and goes as far as to claim he entrapped Eleanor to use her against Louis. 'Raymond resolved to deprive him of his wife,' wrote William, 'either by force or by secret intrigue. The Queen readily assented to this design for she was a foolish woman. Her conduct before and after

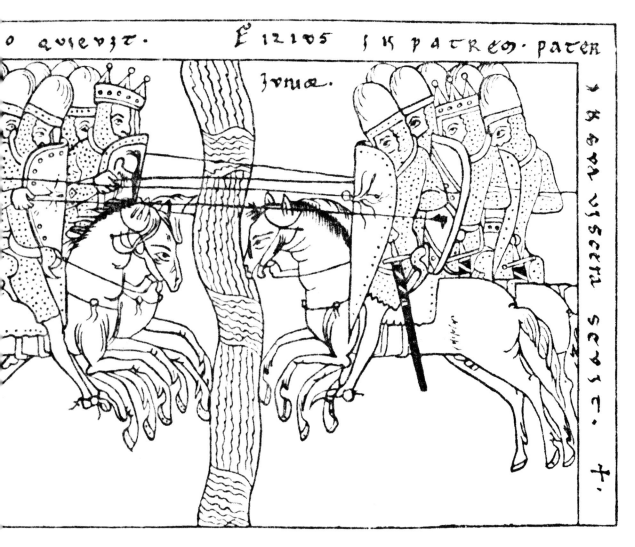

o quievzt.   E 12105   in patreo. pater

Jrua.

German knights battle
across the River Regen.
From the twelfth-century
chronicle of Otto of Freising.

this time showed her to be far from circumspect. Contrary to her dignity,
she disregarded her marriage vows and was unfaithful to her husband.'
Taken from French sources, William's criticism generally reflects French
outrage at Eleanor's independent behaviour, but he counters this by saying
it was the king's fault: Louis should have acceded to Raymond's request, for
Edessa could easily have been taken.

Leaving Antioch abruptly, Louis led his army to Jerusalem and Eleanor
was forced to go with him. The subsequent failure of the expedition did
little to reconcile the rift between the royal couple and they returned to
France in separate ships. While resting in Sicily, Eleanor heard news that
Raymond had been struck down in battle and his blond head delivered to
the Caliph of Baghdad. In Paris, the marriage was restored and Eleanor bore
Louis a second daughter. But the relationship was over and in 1152 the

fideſ peilit diſcordiā figeſſ lancea

ingenti

Honcult ulceri capti blaſphemia monſtri
virtutū regina fideſ. ſ, ūba loquentiſ
Impedit. & uocis claudit ſpiramina pilo.
Pollutā rigida ensfigens cuſpide linguā.
virtutes   ſcinduit   diſcordiam

Women warriors as the personification of faith spearing discord and virtues beheading discord. From an early twelfth-century manuscript of Prudentius's *Psychomachia*.

Eleanor of Aquitaine riding with a companion, probably Isabella of Angoulême. From an early thirteenth-century wall painting in the chapel of St Radegund at Chinon.

marriage annulled. Her extensive estates reverted to her control, but she was too astute to rule independently and risk a war with the King of France. Within the year, she had procured another strong alliance. She married Henry Plantagenet, Count of Anjou and Duke of Normandy. It has been suggested that the idea of this marriage had been conceived the previous year when the Plantagenets visited Paris. Eleanor would not be left alone for long; she made sure of that. Eleanor was 30 and Henry had just turned 20. It was a good choice, for not only did they match each other in power, but their personalities were more alive to each other. Two years later, Henry Plantagenet became Henry II of England. For the second time, Eleanor was queen of a major European power, bringing western France under English authority.

Over the next two decades, Eleanor concentrated on raising her family and creating an active and brilliant court culture centred around Poitiers. She bore Henry five sons and three daughters. The second son became Richard I and the last born was John, also a future King of England. At the age of 50 Eleanor was a powerful stateswoman. She assisted in the running of the Plantagenet domain and was securely in charge of her own estates.

But Eleanor and Henry had grown apart. The king had his mistresses and Eleanor spent most of her time at Poitiers, lavishing her love and wisdom on her sons. In 1173, three of these young men rebelled against their father and took command of their French territories. Henry was suddenly isolated in England and had to recruit an army of mercenaries before he could quell his French subjects. Eleanor did not take the lead in this revolt, but it is felt sure she masterminded it and provided substantial military support. There is even some suggestion that she may have commanded forces in the field. When the rebellion failed and Eleanor rode for sanctuary in the domain of Louis VII, she was captured by Plantagenet knights and found to be wearing male clothing for disguise.

An indication of the degree to which Eleanor was thought responsible for the rebellion was provided by her imprisonment in England. Her husband kept her confined for nearly 15 years. Henry preferred to forgive his sons than his wife. He would also rather have her under lock and key in his own country, than divorced and head of an independent realm in France. Only with the death of Henry in 1189 did Eleanor obtain her freedom. She re-entered the political field with even more vigour. Administering the country while Richard I was on crusade, she raised the ransom for his release from the Duke of Austria and personally escorted him home. In 1199, when John ascended the throne, she was also his greatest supporter, helping him defend his land in France. At almost 80, the future of the English crown still rested with her. She was a remarkable ruler. Even after her death in 1204, her own estates in France remained loyal to the English while Normandy returned to the French.

Hundred Years
War Women

**JEANNE OF
MONTFORT,
CHRISTINE DE
PISAN,
JOAN OF ARC**

Knights brought bad news to Jeanne, Countess of Montfort. Her husband was captured at Nantes by the men of Blois. Amid her anger and fear, the countess calmly reassured her followers. The cause of Montfort was not dead. She would carry on her husband's work and bring the whole of Brittany under the rule of Montfort. Within her residence at Rennes, she presented her young boy to her husband's supporters and men-at-arms.

'Gentlemen,' she said, 'do not be cast down by the loss of my lord. He is but one man. Look at my little son here. If it please God, he shall restore our rule and shall do you much service. I have great wealth and will distribute it among you. I shall then seek out a leader in which you will have confidence.'

Her words of assurance restored the morale of the Montfort cause and she proceeded to all the towns and castles in Brittany still under her command, showing them her son and convincing them of the need to continue the struggle. She strengthened her garrisons with both men and provisions, using her money generously to gain whatever was needed. During the winter, she retired to Hennebont, near the south Breton coast, making frequent excursions to her fortresses to ensure her men were well paid and supplied. Froissart, the chronicler of these events, was highly impressed by the countess. 'She possessed the courage of a man and the heart of a lion,' he exclaimed. The leader she had spoken of in her speech was herself.

The civil war in Brittany had broken out in 1341. It was a war over succession to the duchy. Philip VI, King of France, favoured Charles of Blois as the new duke—his wife had been niece to the previous ruler. But John of Montfort, half-brother to the late duke, believed he had the superior claim. In a lightning campaign that summer, John of Montfort usurped Charles of Blois and plunged the duchy into civil war. With the support of the King of France, Charles of Blois invaded Brittany in the autumn. Closing in on Nantes, John of Montfort's headquarters, the native Bretons were anxious about the combat. Two armies battling for succession had little respect for the common property of ordinary Bretons. The citizens of Nantes were particularly concerned about their own fate during a siege. Fearing the greater force of the King of France, they made a secret treaty with Charles of Blois by which they would be spared the ravages of a siege if Blois's men were allowed into the town to attack Montfort's castle. Through this treachery, Montfort was quickly captured, leaving his wife to continue the war.

With her husband in prison in Paris, the Countess of Montfort needed a powerful ally. She turned to Edward III, King of England, and promised her son in marriage to one of his daughters. Seeing a good opportunity to strengthen his grip over western France, Edward sent Sir Walter Mauny with a contingent of men-at-arms and 6,000 archers. A great storm kept the fleet at sea for 40 days. It was a crucial delay. While the countess celebrated the support of Edward at Hennebont, Charles of Blois chose the summer of 1342 for his final campaign of conquest. Leading a large French army and mercenaries from Spain and Genoa, he moved against Rennes. Froissart writes that the countess had well fortified the town and placed a Breton, Sir William de Cadoudal, in command. To begin with, the French made furious assaults on its walls and were beaten back, suffering severe losses. But the citizens of Rennes had less confidence in the outcome than their captain and began to suggest capitulation. Sir William refused, but Blois kept up the pressure and the citizens of Rennes turned on their captain and flung him into prison. With the assurance that members of the Montfort party would be unharmed, Rennes opened its gates to Blois. Sir William rode back to Hennebont, where the countess had still not received news of the English army.

Church bells rang out the alarm that Charles of Blois would follow his success at Rennes by attacking Hennebont. Inside the town walls, the countess was surrounded by her most loyal knights: Sir William de Cadoudal, Sir Galeran de Landreman, Sir Yves de Tresiquidi, and the brothers Sir Oliver and Sir Henry de Spinefort. Outside the walls, Charles of Blois encamped his men and made preparations for the siege. On the first day, the young and most daring men-at-arms among the French, Spaniards and Genoese crossed the barriers between their camp and the town walls to skirmish with the defenders. It was a typical first step. Not so much a serious assault as an attempt to judge the ferocity of the defenders and maybe win a few reputations for aspiring knights. Rising to the challenge, the Bretons gave them a tough fight, the Genoese losing more casualties than they inflicted.

On the second day, the Countess of Montfort had a suit of armour brought to her. With its mail shirt and iron plates strapped on, she rode a war-horse through the streets of Hennebont, encouraging the citizens to defend themselves. She ordered the women of the town to remove rocks and stones from buildings and throw them down on the enemy from the walls. Pots of quicklime were also flung from the ramparts. She then ascended a tower on the wall and noted the positions of the enemy. The

'Scythian women on the attack', from the thirteenth-century *Histoire Universelle*, now in the British Library, London. The scene represents a favourite theatrical entertainment of crusader warlords in Syria, the re-enactment of famous episodes from history, such as the triumph of the Amazons, or it may allude to the presence of women crusaders.

lune royne requirra quant elles su
rent uengieo ⁊ lautir rimeſt eu gce.

Ntre elles auoit .ij. amis.
roynes. lune anomoit mer
pſia. ⁊ lautre lampeto. Jueneo da
mes ⁊ belleo de coro ⁊ de uiſageo ⁊
de cuer hardies. Ceſteo furent mlt
bien atozner leur afaureo. ſi come
poz cheuauchier aforce ſur leur
annemis. ⁊ leur terreo conquerre.
Qdaio anſois q̈lleo iſſiſſent ⁊ depar
tiſſent de leur contireo: occiſtrent
elleo too les homeo ⁊ leo enfano
maſleo. poz q̈lleo ſe concozdaſcet
miauo enſemble a vne uoléte ſaz
reteaure. Pont ni ot pluo. riche
ment atozneeo ⁊ apparreilliee ſe
miſtrent alauoie. ⁊tant aleirent q̈
elleo entreirent en la terre aleur an
nemio. ou elleo ueugierent bien
loz gr̄t duloz. Car as aro ⁊ as ſe
eteo ⁊ao eſpeo eſmoluveo deſtrui
rent elleo leur annemis. Coment

Nſi ⁊ pur ceſte achaiſon co
menſierent premieremet
les dameo en celle region a pozter
aumeo. q̈ puio deuindrent mlt
uaillanz ⁊mlt cheualeruſeo. ſi
come uoo pozeo cil uoo plaiſt a
uant oïr ⁊ entendre. Apres ceſte
premerarme bataille q̈lleo ozent
deſconfite ⁊ uentue: leo .ij. royneo
merpſia ⁊ lampete: deuiſierent loz
compaigunie en .ij. purtieo. ⁊ ſire
paurr lune atoteo ſeo damoiſelleo
en leur terre poz garder la countree.
⁊ lautre atoteo ſeo gr̄z compai
gineo priſt la cuir de la bataille poz
prio ⁊ poz le tiru deo grenz deo eſtrā
geo contreeo auoir ⁊ conq̈rre. En
ſi le fauſoient leo roÿneo a la foice.
⁊ celleo q̈ loz regneo gardoient: ſi
cozdoient as eſtrangeo homeo q̈
preo delleo eſtoient qr̄t il loz plai

majority of Blois's army had joined together in a major assault on the town, leaving their camp exposed. Gathering 300 horsemen, she broke out from a gate along a stretch of the wall not under assault. Dashing past bewildered scouts and guards, the countess led her gang of horsemen straight into the deserted encampment. Only a few servants and stable-boys leapt to their feet, but were instantly cut down. Hurling flaming torches into the empty tents, the camp was enveloped in fire. Drawn by the clouds of smoke and cries of 'treason!', the French abandoned the assault to save their camp. The route back to Hennebont was now cut off and the countess urged her horsemen out of the burning camp on to the road towards the castle of Brest. Lewis of Spain, marshal of Blois's army, ordered a large body of men-at-arms to pursue the countess. The chase was hard and furious through the Breton forest and many of the countess's less well-mounted followers fell victim to the angry hunters, but the countess and a few men outdistanced the French and made it to Brest.

For five days, the citizens of Hennebont heard nothing of their countess. Their morale was low and there was talk of surrender. But the countess's knights kept faith and waited. Their trust was justified. At the end of the week, she returned under cover of midnight with 600 newly recruited men-at-arms. To a blast of trumpets, the countess re-entered Hennebont at sunrise. The French awoke with a start and began another assault on the walls. The fighting continued until past midday, but the French were losing too many troops to make it worth carrying on. Charles of Blois had had enough. He left a good part of the Spanish and Genoese, under Sir Hervé de Léon and Lewis of Spain, to continue the siege, and rode away with the majority of the French soldiers to attack the castle of Auray. There were now too few warriors to take Hennebont by assault, but the Spanish commanders called up 12 siege machines from Rennes to annoy the citizens by casting huge boulders among them. It was a victory of a kind for the countess, but she was still penned in her fortress with no sign of English reinforcements.

The siege machines began to make an impact. The walls of Hennebont crumbled and so did the morale of its defenders. Among the noblemen in the Countess of Montfort's castle was the Bishop of Léon, uncle of Sir Hervé de Léon, one of the enemy commanders. He asked permission to speak to his nephew to resolve the siege. But as soon as he was in the enemy camp, he revealed the despair of the townspeople and agreed to try and win them over so as to open its gates on the promise of a pardon from Charles of Blois. When the bishop returned to Hennebont, the countess was suspicious and begged her knights not to be talked into surrender. She promised the English would come within a few days, but the bishop spoke so convincingly of good terms with Blois that the noblemen were unsure what to do. In the meantime, Sir Hervé de Léon prepared his army to take control of the town. The countess retired to a tower in her castle and wept. Through the window, she glimpsed the sails of a great fleet. Townsfolk were called to the walls and they also saw the sails. It was the English army promised by King Edward.

The Breton knights reaffirmed their support to the countess. The Bishop of Léon admitted his true loyalties and left for the enemy camp. Sir Hervé was furious. He placed his largest trebuchet close to the countess's castle and hurled stones at it day and night. The countess prepared her quarters for a grand reception. Tapestries were hung in her chambers and animals slaughtered. From Froissart's description, it appears the siege was not an all-encompassing one. The enemy was close enough to keep the citizens at arms, but not big enough to prevent the coming and going of troops and supplies. Sir Walter Mauny and his several thousand soldiers entered Hennebont without any trouble from the besiegeing army. That night, as the countess and the English celebrated their alliance, Sir Walter Mauny stood at a window and looked out at the great siege machine. Its pounding against the castle walls all evening greatly annoyed him.

'If anyone will second me,' he announced, 'I will silence that irritation.'

Sir Yves de Tresiquidi and Sir Galeran de Landreman stepped forward. With 300 archers and men-at-arms, the English and Breton knights crept out. Their archers scattered the guards protecting the trebuchet and the men-at-arms broke it up. They then dashed among the camp of the enemy and set their tents alight. The French leapt to their horses and chased the raiders. Seeing his pursuers, Sir Walter Mauny turned his horse to face them.

'May I never be embraced by my mistress and dear friend,' he vowed, 'if I enter that castle without first dismounting one of these horsemen.'

He then lowered his lance and charged the enemy. The Breton knights rallied to his defence and a fierce combat broke out before the moat of the town. Citizens of Hennebont spilled out to join in the battle. Their archery forced the enemy to retreat. Back inside the town, the countess came out of her castle and greeted the victorious warriors, kissing Sir Walter Mauny and his knight comrades.

The destruction of their siege machines was the last straw for Lewis of Spain and Sir Hervé de Léon. They could see the garrison was too strong to be overcome. They broke up their camp and led the Genoese and Spanish mercenaries to Charles of Blois at Auray. The citizens of Hennebont rushed out after the retreating army, but lost many lives in their eagerness to humiliate them. From Auray, Lewis of Spain was sent to take the castle of Conquet and then besiege Dinan. The war was essentially a series of sieges, for whoever held the towns of Brittany controlled the land and stood closer to claiming the dukedom. The countess sent Sir Walter Mauny after Lewis of Spain and he recaptured the castle of Conquet. But the Spaniard was a professional warlord and went on to storm Dinan and Guerrande. The sacking of these towns was ferocious and the Spanish and Genoese can have won little support among the Bretons. Eventually, Lewis packed his booty on a fleet of ships and set sail for further adventure at sea.

Throughout the summer of 1342, the English forces of Montfort and the French forces of Blois captured town after town across Brittany. But no one seemed any closer to outright victory. Such was the stalemate that the King of England, on the advice of Sir Walter Mauny, urged the Countess of Montfort and Charles of Blois to agree a truce. It may be that Blois found himself in a stronger position, for after the truce was concluded, the Countess of Montfort left Brittany for England. It is also possible that the countess wished to thank the king personally for his assistance and try to persuade him she was worth backing again. The truce expired in the spring of 1343 and the countess's arguments appear to have won through. At the head of an English fleet, including Robert of Artois, the Earls of Pembroke, Salisbury, Suffolk, Oxford and many other notable knights, she returned to Brittany.

Just off Guernsey, Lewis of Spain waited for the English. He commanded 32 ships carrying 3,000 Genoese crossbowmen and 1,000 men-at-arms. The English had 46 vessels, but they were lighter than the Spaniard's ships, especially his three massive galleys. Lewis sailed in one galley, while his two other captains, Sir Charles Grimaldi and Sir Otho Doria, commanded the others. The English had the wind with them and when they saw the apparently smaller Spanish fleet, they attacked. Trumpets blaring, pennons fluttering, and the banner of St George unfurled, the English ships set full sail for the enemy. The Countess of Montfort wore a suit of armour at the helm of her ship and wielded a sword. As the fleets approached, the English bowmen exchanged volleys with the Genoese crossbowmen.

In close combat, the superior size of the Spanish ships proved an advantage. Genoese and Spanish troops dropped great bars of iron on to the decks of the English ships and stabbed at their men-at-arms with long lances. Towards the end of the afternoon, a fog rose, forcing the ships to break. The two fleets cast anchor and prepared to continue the battle the next day. But the fog was followed by a severe storm in the night. The English set their smaller, frailer vessels towards land, while the Spaniards weathered the storm in their larger ships. As the two fleets passed each other in the stormy night, the Spaniards managed to sieze four English ships laden with provisions. The next day, neither fleet could see the other.

The English disembarked on the beach near Vannes and immediately set siege to it. Robert of Artois appears to have been the chief commander of the English army, but when the town was assaulted, the Countess of Montfort rode joyfully at his side as they entered it. From Vannes, the countess returned to Hennebont, held by Sir Walter Mauny while she was in England. The main English force set siege to Rennes. A little later, the French regained Vannes. And so, the indecisiveness continued. Towards the end of the year, the King of England joined in the fighting, landing near Vannes and again laying siege to it. This was an important escalation in the war. It encouraged the French king to send the duke of Normandy to assist Charles of Blois. The situation was now getting beyond the control of the

Town under siege, from an early fifteenth-century manuscript.

Countess of Montfort. By the end of the year, Pope Clermont VI had sent two cardinals to bring some sense to the warring factions. A truce of three years was agreed upon. The war in Brittany had become part of a greater conflict between the Kings of England and France that would eventually merge into the opening rounds of the Hundred Years War. The Countess of Montfort was no longer fighting for her husband's cause, but was part of a greater strategy in which the King of England held ultimate authority. From Froissart, we hear that the countess was entrusted by the King of England to her leading Breton knights in order to keep the peace, while Edward built up his forces for a second assault on France. In the meantime, the King of France grew suspicious of the failure of his knights in Brittany and had

119

many of them executed, encouraging some of their descendants to side with the Countess of Montfort. While the countess waited for her next instructions from the King of England, news came through of her husband's death in Paris.

The truce in Brittany was strictly observed, although in the same three years, Edward invaded Gascony and Normandy and defeated the French soundly at the Battle of Crécy. With the English in ascendancy, the Countess of Montfort emerged from her retirement with vigour. In the summer of 1347, the King of England sent Sir Thomas Daggeworth and Sir John Hartwell into Brittany with 200 men-at-arms and 400 archers. They were ordered to harry the forces of Charles of Blois. Rampaging through Brittany, they overturned the reconstruction begun in the years of truce. 'The country was completely ruined by these men-at-arms,' wrote Froissart, 'and the poor people paid dearly for it.' From Hennebont, the Countess of Montfort and Sir Taneguy du Chatel, a knight from lower Brittany, joined in the war of attrition against Blois. A major confrontation developed at La Roche Derrien in northern Brittany.

The captain of the garrison at La Roche Derrien was Sir Tassart de Guines, a support of Charles of Blois. The townspeople were less persuaded by his cause and did not want to embroil themselves in a siege. They were happy to accede to English demands. Sir Tassart ignored their views at his peril. They arrested him and threatened death unless he surrendered the town to the English. Throughout the Breton civil war, the ordinary Bretons did not care who ruled over them so long as they were left alone to enjoy a relatively peaceful life. As a result, the English entered the town and placed their soldiers there. Sir Tassart was allowed to remain in command, revealing the fluid loyalties of Breton knights. He probably realised the conflict was part of a much larger power-play and considered it sensible to swing with the blows. Charles of Blois could not afford to be so easy: behind him was the King of France. La Roche Derrien could not be allowed to fall into English hands.

From Brittany and Normandy, Charles recruited 400 knights, 1,600 men-at-arms, and 12,000 foot-soldiers. From Nantes, they marched northwards, bringing with them several siege machines with wagons full of stones. The citizens of La Roche Derrien could see they had now brought an even bigger problem to their walls. They sent messengers to the Countess of Montfort, asking her for the assistance she had promised. She assembled 1,000 men-at-arms and 8,000 foot-soldiers and sent them under the command of Sir Thomas Daggeworth and Sir John Hartwell. Taking up quarters outside La Roche Derrien, on the banks of a river near to Blois's forces camped beside the town, the English knights prepared half their army for a night assault on the French encampment. Around midnight, they crept across the black fields and descended on the flank of Blois's soldiers. The fighting went well for them, but the rest of the French were roused from their sleep and joined in. Their superior numbers overwhelmed the English and they were surrounded. After being severely wounded, Sir Thomas Daggeworth was taken prisoner. Sir John Hartwell just managed to escape along the river. Back in the English camp, he recommended Sir Taneguy du Chatel to give up and return to Hennebont.

Into this war council strode Sir William de Cadoudal with 100 men-at-arms. He had just arrived from the countess and would not brook defeat so soon.

'Arm yourselves quickly,' he urged, 'mount your horses. The enemy shall be defeated all the more easily now they are elated with victory.'

At sunrise, the English and Bretons charged into the camp of the exhausted French, cut down their tents and slew their warriors. So confident had they been in their victory over the English, they had not bothered to station their usual guards. It was an easy triumph. The English knights rode up to the tent of Charles of Blois and took him prisoner. The surprised lord was carried back to Hennebont, where the countess could gloat with satisfaction at the defeat of her husband's adversary. It might be thought this would bring an end to the civil war, but there were far more powerful interests involved which could not allow the war to end. Just as the countess had found the English ready to back her, so the French pledged their support to Blois's wife, Joan of Penthièvre. It was under her that the war would continue for many more years until the English and French felt ready to make terms. The Countess of Montfort's personal victory could not be allowed to finish the fighting.

It was only after another 20 years, in 1366, that a new French king, Charles V, was ready to accept the Countess of Montfort's son as the new Duke of Brittany. Nothing else is heard of the countess in Froissart's chronicles after 1347. Recent scholars of the chronicler have disputed the countess's involvement in events after 1343. It is believed that when she left Brittany with Edward III in February of that year, she never returned, but lived the rest of her life in exile in England. As to her husband John, he is believed not to have died in prison in Paris, but escaped to England in 1345 to make homage to Edward. He then returned to Brittany with Sir William Bohun, Earl of Northampton, only to die shortly after from disease. Whatever the contrary views of Froissart's history, the truth of the Countess of Montfort's commanding role in the war remains. She did emerge as the leading member of the Montfort faction in Brittany in the early years of the civil war and conducted her task successfully.

The Countess of Montfort's commanding role in the affairs of Brittany would have been no surprise to Christine de Pisan. A French author of the early fifteenth century, Christine encouraged women to be in charge of their own lives. In her *Treasure of the City of Ladies*, written in 1405, she advises a noblewoman how to govern her lands when her husband dies. 'First, she must understand thoroughly the last will and testament of her husband,' she recommended. 'If anyone tries to cheat her out of what belongs to her—as often happens to widowed ladies—she must summon good assistance to protect her rights boldly by law and reason.' A noblewoman will further good government in her realm by acting as a mediator between her barons and try to reconcile any differences between them. 'But if her land is attacked by foreign enemies—as frequently happens after the death of a prince with under-age children—it will be necessary for her to make and conduct war. She must keep the good will of her barons and lords so they are loyal and come to the aid of her child. She must also have the service of knights, squires, and gentlemen so they will boldly fight for their young lord. She must keep the affection of the people too, in order to help with her wealth and property. She must speak to her subjects, so they will not betray her, saying that the great expense of war will not, if it pleases God, last long.' It is the kind of scenario that applied to the Countess of Montfort and her example along with other noblewomen during the Hundred Years War may well have inspired Christine.

Christine de Pisan's call for female independence emanates from her own experience. Her father and husband died shortly after her marriage, leaving her at 25 to support three children and her mother. With no trade to follow and no wish to remarry or enter a convent, Christine began a career of her own. While she studied history and developed literary skills, she was compelled to fight four law suits concurrently to ensure her rightful inheritance. The final settlements were never enough to support her and her family, but her writing became popular at the courts of France and England and she enjoyed a prosperous celebrity as a writer of poetry, history and sound advice. The sad, harsh reality of her widowhood gave her a great respect for other women who had overcome the prejudice and persecution of a male-dominated world. In her *City of Ladies*, written in 1404, she argued against the vilification of women, then in vogue among male writers. She quoted examples of women past and present who demonstrated qualities of intelligence, creativity and moral virtue. She cited the Amazons, Zenobia and several medieval French queens as strong, capable female rulers. At the end of her book, she places all these famous women behind the battlements and towers of her ideal city, saying that it is a refuge for all worthy women and they must defend it against their male enemies.

Such was Christine's confidence in the contribution of women to all the arts and sciences that she had few doubts about writing her own manual on the art of war. In her introduction to *Feats of Arms and Chivalry*, she admits that women are not accustomed to writing on this subject, being more used to matters of the household, but she justifies her interest by invoking the spiritual help of Minerva, Goddess of War. Compiling the most useful elements from ancient Roman military authors—Vegetius, Frontinus and Valerius Maximus—along with contemporary work by Honoré Bonet, she added her own remarks and observations. In her sections on contemporary warfare, she describes the desired qualities of good commanders and soldiers, the best way to choose a campsite and the gathering of stores for a

campaign. She called upon contributions from anonymous knights, gathered at first-hand, and lists the necessary items for an assault on a castle. She begins by recommending two great siege engines and two catapults; four *Coyllardes* machines for hurling iron balls; four great guns named *Garyte*,

Rose, *Senecque* and *Maye*: the first casting about 500 pounds' (230 kg) weight, the second about 400 pounds (180 kg) and the other two about 200 pounds (90 kg); another gun called *Mountfort* casting 300 pounds (140 kg); a brass gun called *Artycke* casting 100-pound (45 kg) weight; 20 smaller guns casting stone pellets; several other small guns casting pellets of lead and stone of 100-pound (45 kg) weight; two great bombards and six smaller ones. The list goes on to describe 34 small and big guns. She then mentions 3,000 pounds (1,360 kg) of gunpowder, plus 3,000 sacks of charcoal from the willow tree and 2,000 sacks of charcoal made from oak trees; 30 charcoal burner's tripods; 30 bellows; 400 or 500 wooden wads for ramming down the barrel between charge and shot; long carts to transport the guns, their powder and other equipment, plus an extra 25 short carts, each pulled by three horses. The list of ordnance carries on to mention mantles for the guns, carts and boats for transport, supplies of wood, crossbows, tools for craftsmen, and stones rounded and ready for guns and catapults. The list is exhaustive and detailed. Clearly, Christine had gone to great pains to get the facts of contemporary warfare correct so that her book would be a useful manual for commanding officers. In her introduction, she emphasised her determination to write in a plain language, for warriors are not clerks. Such was the usefulness of this manual that, 80 years later, Henry VII instructed William Caxton to translate it into English for his commanders.

For all Christine's familiarity with the detail of war, she is all the more determined that it should be avoided. Throughout her books she advises negotiation and reconciliation, the use of impartial counsellors. God condemns wars of vengeance and aggression, she says. But in her introduction to *Feats of Arms and Chivalry*, she does admit occasions permitted by God in which a land and its people should be lawfully protected against oppression and that a prince may take up arms to obtain justice for himself.

In the wake of Agincourt and towards the end of her life, Christine retired to a convent. Ten years earlier, she had warned the French queen that if her princes continued their civil war, then their kingdom would be vulnerable to foreign invasion. Her prophecy had come true and she now devoted herself to writing prayers for women who lost their husbands in the war. Shortly before her death, around 1429, Christine wrote a short poem, a Hymn to Joan of Arc. The teenage heroine had just raised the siege of Orleans and led the dauphin, Charles, to his coronation at Rheims. 'What an honour for the female sex,' she wrote, 'which God so loves that he showed a way to this great people by which the kingdom, once lost, was recovered by a woman. A thing that men could not do.' For Christine, Joan was the epitome of all that she had written about. At the end of her poem, she hoped that Joan would lead the French king on a crusade to the Holy Land. It is the only contemporary tribute to Joan to have survived.

Unlike all previous women warlords discussed, Joan of Arc did not rise to power because of the loss of a husband. At the age of 16, in 1428, Joan was

Early wheeled cannon employed against a castle, detail from a mid-fifteenth-century manuscript.

dazzled by a bright light in her father's garden. The heavenly voices of Saints Michael, Margaret and Catherine spoke to her. They instructed her to help the King of France and raise the English siege of Orleans. But how could she do that, she asked, she was just a peasant girl who knew neither how to ride nor lead men in battle. The voices told her to go to Robert de Baudricourt, captain of the royal garrison at Vaucouleurs. He would provide her with soldiers. And so she embarked on the brief military career that won France a significant triumph in the Hundred Years War and ensured her fame as the most celebrated woman warlord.

If the facts of Joan's military success were not attested by essentially reliable contemporary records, it would be difficult to believe the reality of her leadership. For a peasant girl to rise rapidly to the position of *chef de guerre* of the royal French army and lead them to victory is perhaps the most remarkable military career ever. The immediate explanation for her success seems to lie in the dire situation of the French royal party. In the early 1420s, the English and Burgundians had united against the French king and conquered most of northern France, including Paris. In such a situation, any new military solution, however eccentric, must have been welcomed by the unconsecrated King Charles VII, also called the dauphin. And yet, the men convinced by Joan's claims were war-hardened professional soldiers. Not surprisingly, on her first visit to the veteran Baudricourt, the answer was to send the girl back to her father with a clip round the ear. On a second visit to Vaucouleurs in 1429, the French position was even worse and only Orleans remained a pocket of resistance north of the Loire. One of Baudricourt's knights, Jean de Metz, was in the mood for listening to Joan's claims and promised to take her to the king. He was her first convert. Baudricourt remained sceptical and had a priest exorcise her of any evil spirits, but he was now beginning to respond to the girl in the mystical manner necessary for her triumph. Word of her spiritual claims reached the dying Duke of Lorraine and his request to see her added to her credibility. Baudricourt provided her with a horse, man's clothing and an escort of six soldiers, including Jean de Metz. At first, the escort thought she was not completely sane, but by the end of the journey Jean de Metz was 'on fire with her words and a divine love for her. I believe she was sent by God.'

Several female mystics had been received at the courts of France throughout the previous century. Charles VI had given time to Marie Robine, a woman from Avignon, who believed she was a prophetess. According to Jean Erault, a professor of theology, Marie experienced a vision in which she saw 'pieces of armour brought before her. She was afraid to put them on, but was told it was not her who would have to wear the armour, but a Maid who would come after her and deliver the kingdom of France from its enemies.' In this climate of expectation, even the University of Paris appealed in 1413 to all those possessing the gift of prophecy to come forward and deliver the kingdom of France. Charles VII was himself a pious man who frequently consulted astrologers. After having Joan questioned by royal councillors, the king granted her an audience. Before him, Joan retained her remarkable self-confidence and promised to deliver Orleans and escort him to Rheims, where he would be consecrated as 'lieutenant of the King of Heaven, who is King of France'. Pleased by her devout words and earnest proclamations, Charles gave her lodgings in his castle at Chinon.

Neither embarrassed by the presence of men nor physically shy of violent activity, the teenage Joan amused herself at Chinon by tilting at the quintain. As she awaited the king's decision, several lords and knights conversed with her. The most impressed of these was the Duke of Alençon, himself in his mid-twenties. After watching her practise with a lance, he gave her a war-horse. Before giving her royal patronage, the king, on the advice of his council, asked Joan to attend a three-week trial at Poitiers. There, under the examination of several prominent churchmen, Joan maintained her desire to free Orleans from English siege. The examiners asked her for a sign of her heavenly mission, but Joan insisted that this would be proved at Orleans so long as she was given the soldiers to help her. A physical examination established that she was indeed a woman and a virgin. The latter was deemed important as a woman without her virginity could be a witch. The result of the trial was that Joan was judged a good, true, pure and Christian person.

Subsequently, Joan was given the title of *chef de guerre*. The king provided her with a suit of armour, a squire, two pages and two heralds. At Tours she had two banners painted. The larger one, her personal standard, had the image of God seated in judgement among clouds with an angel holding a fleur-de-lys in his hand which the image was blessing. To the right of the image were the words *Jhesus Maria*, the whole set against a white background decorated with fleurs-de-lys. A smaller pennon, perhaps her company's standard, portrayed the Annunciation with a dove carrying a scroll with the words 'on behalf of the King of Heaven'. Her sword was not made for her, but in true heroic fashion, found buried behind the altar of the church of Saint Catherine at Fierbois. The rusty blade had five crosses engraved on it. But her sword was of little importance to her. Later, at her trial before the English, she said she preferred her standard to her sword and 'bore it when we went forward against the enemy to avoid killing anyone. I have never killed anyone.' Her most valuable weapon, as far as the French were concerned, was her charismatic leadership.

In April 1429, Joan was 17. At the head of some 4,000 men-at-arms and archers, she left Blois, on the north bank of the Loire, and rode towards Orleans. A company of priests marched before her, singing the '*Veni Creator Spiritus*'. She dispatched a letter to the English commanders at Orleans and their king, saying: 'I have been sent by God, the king of Heaven, to drive you, body for body, out of all France. If you do not believe this news sent to you by God and the Maid, we will strike you, wherever we find you, and make such a great attack that France has not seen in a thousand years.' The English sent no reply and held her herald, making the point that they did not consider her a true commander, subject to military law. Throughout her military career, Joan was known as *la Pucelle*, or the Maid, and it was only late in the sixteenth century that she gained her surname d'Arc. The extent to which Joan was in command of the French army marching towards Orleans is in dispute. It is tempting to regard her simply as a useful figurehead. Count Dunois, the Bastard of Orleans, was the dominant French commander of the campaign. He had been in charge of the town's defences for six months. Her title *chef de guerre* may well have been just an official formula inserted as a matter of course in letters to the English command. But on later occasions, French military captains bore witness to her innate skills of command.

'Apart from the matter of war, she was simple and ignorant,' stated the knight Thibaud d'Armagnac. 'But in the conduct and disposition of armies, in their drawing up in battle order and the raising of soldiers' morale, she behaved as if she had been the shrewdest captain in the world and had all her life been learning the art of war.' The Duke of Alençon, a veteran commander and organiser of her supply train at Blois, was impressed by her 'management of the lance in drawing up the army in battle order and in the preparing of artillery. All marvelled that she could act in so prudent and well-advised a fashion as might a captain of twenty or thirty years experience, especially in the preparation of artillery.' He adds also that her chaste character had a deep influence on himself and his soldiers. 'Whenever I saw her,' he recalled, 'I refrained from my swearing. And sometimes on campaign when we lay down to sleep together I saw Joan prepare for the night and saw her breasts, which were beautiful, and yet I never had a carnal desire for her.'

Arriving at Orleans, Joan approached from the south bank, with the River Loire between her and the town. This was Dunois's idea, as the safest passage for the supplies she brought lay across the river into the town. Joan was furious, revealing her belief that she was in command of the relief operation, not him. 'Did you give counsel that I should come here and not go straight to the English?' she asked Dunois. 'In God's name, the counsel of the Lord your God is wiser and safer than yours.' At that moment, a wind rose on the river, easing the passage of her supply boats into the town. Using this as his excuse for accepting her divine inspiration, Dunois encouraged her first to enter the besieged town across the river by the eastern Burgundy Gate, the one entrance under least control by the English. Reluctantly, Joan followed him.

The English had held their positions on the north bank, outside Orleans, for seven months with an army of around 5,000 English and Burgundians. The English had command of the western approaches to the town and stormed Les Tournelles, a stone fortress commanding the south-bank entrance to a bridge crossing the Loire into Orleans. The English captains were Sir John Talbot and Sir Thomas Scales. They had a ring of small fortresses converted from buildings and churches about 550 yards (500 m) from the town walls. Dunois had ordered the destruction of much of this cover in the suburbs, forcing the English to raise new forts to blockade the roads into the town. The siege was not complete and supplies occasionally broke through. A regular bombardment was maintained by the English artillery and there were several skirmishes, but the English were reluctant

Brigandine of the fifteenth century, a flexible armour of metal plates secured beneath a cloth coat by rivets, now in the Tower of London.

to attempt a direct assault. The population of the town was at least 20,000 strong and there was probably a garrison with militia of around 4,000 at the time of Joan's arrival. Added to this was a formidable artillery of 71 guns mounted on the walls. One of these cannon had sent a ball against the English in Les Tournelles and struck the Earl of Salisbury in the face, wounding the English commander so badly that he died a few days later. Shortly before the arrival of Joan, the English had also suffered the loss of their Burgundian allies, because of a political argument, and had to continue the siege alone.

Joan's entry into Orleans was stage-managed perfectly. In the evening, with skirmishing diverting the attention of the English, Joan rode through the eastern Burgundy Gate. She wore full armour and sat upon a white

129

horse. Her white standard, bearing the image of the Lord, was carried before her. At her left side rode Count Dunois. Behind them came the other commanders and knights. Despite the late hour, the people of Orleans surged out of their houses to greet the Maid. They held their torches close to the welcome party and one of their flaming lights sparked against the standard, setting it on fire. Joan spurred her horse forward and grabbed the standard to extinguish it. Her confident action impressed the crowd even more and they followed her to her quarters.

Having successfully used Joan to raise the spirits of the townspeople, Dunois was reluctant to expose her to any further action. Not all Joan's army followed her into Orleans and it was Dunois who rode out to bring the rest of them to the town. Joan, meanwhile, rode around the town, inspecting the enemy's positions. She shouted to some of the English across the defences, telling them to leave at once. She received only insults, being told she was nothing but 'a whore and should go back to minding her cows'. With the return of Dunois and the rest of her soldiers, Joan's patience was running thin. Again, Dunois appears to have held overall command and refused to divulge his plans. After one dinner with the French commander, Joan told him she had heard that English reinforcements were expected and that unless he told her of their arrival, 'I promise you I will have your head chopped off.' Dunois responded politely but clearly had little faith in her as an active military leader.

That same night, the unsettled Joan left her bed and called her squire to fit her armour. Her belief that fighting was going on outside the town walls was confirmed by the sound of action beyond the eastern gate. Without telling her, Dunois had begun an assault on the weakest part of the English lines, the fortified church of St Loup, 1 mile (2 km) east of the Burgundy Gate. It was Joan's first experience of battle and the sight of wounded Frenchmen horrified and saddened her. But she urged her horse on and joined the attack just as a contingent of English arrived to reinforce the defenders of St Loup. Seeing Joan and her standard, the French troops gave a great shout and stormed the church.

Dunois was impressed by Joan's involvement in the night assault and included her in a council of war alongside the other captains present. The decision was made to attack Les Tournelles on the bridge across the Loire. One chronicler, however, states that Joan was called late to the meeting and assigned the role of a diversionary attack. There is no other evidence of this and, the following day, she rode out of the Burgundy Gate with Dunois, La Hire, Gilles de Rais and 4,000 men-at-arms. The assault on Les Tournelles was complicated by several layers of fortification. A small fortress, called St Jean-le-Blanc, stood to the east of the bridgehead and a fortified monastery to the south of it. The tower itself was protected by earthworks, a palisade and moat. From the Burgundy Gate, the French crossed the river at a shallow point to the little Ile des Toiles. They then rode over a pontoon bridge on to the south bank. The English at St Jean-le-Blanc retreated to the

monastery. An advance group of French soldiers noted the strength of the English in the monastery and turned to inform the main body of their army. The English seized upon their turned backs and broke out from the monastery, engaging them in a mêlée. Joan and La Hire had just arrived with their horses in a boat across the river. Unable to restrain herself any more, she led a band of knights and men-at-arms into the fight. They pushed the English back behind their palisaded defences, but a particularly strong Englishman prevented them entering. Joan's squire pointed the stubborn warrior out to an expert handgunner in the French army. Jean the

Lorrainer raised the muzzle of his primitive gun and, with one well-aimed blast, felled the Englishman. The French rushed into the monastery, forcing the English to the defences on the bridge around Les Tournelles. As night fell and the French consolidated their gains, a messenger told Joan that Dunois had decided to wait for reinforcements before pressing the attack any further. 'You have had your council,' she replied, 'and I have had mine. And believe me, the counsel of the Lord will be carried out and your counsel will perish.'

Early on the morning of 7 May, Joan gathered a party of soldiers and townsmen and made to ride out of the Burgundy Gate. Dunois's second-in-command refused her exit. Joan's warriors threatened him and he let them pass. They crossed the river to the monastery. Joan called upon all the knights present to assist her and together they assaulted the defences around Les Tournelles on three sides. The fighting was bitter and the English hurled everything at hand from the top of their ramparts. Early in the assault, Joan was struck in the shoulder by an arrow. She was afraid and wept, but when some soldiers suggested treating her wound with a spell, she said 'I would rather die than accept a sin against the will of God.' With Joan out of the action, Dunois wanted to bring the assault to an end. But Joan insisted and the French returned to the attack. As the afternoon closed with the English continuing their stiff resistance, Joan mounted her horse and made a short prayer in a nearby vineyard. She then seized her standard and dashed to the edge of the English moat. 'When the wind blows the flag towards the rampart,' she cried, 'the fortress will be yours.' With a simultaneous attack from militiamen rowing across the river and raising ladders against the broken bridge on the northern side, the French threw themselves across the ramparts and forced the English out of the tower. Several drowned in the river as they attempted to escape and none of their commanding officers survived—all were slaughtered in the fury. It was a remarkable victory: due solely to Joan's charismatic presence. If it had been left to Dunois, the French may eventually have won, but it would have taken weeks of counter-siege. Within days, the shock of defeat and the loss of their strategic foothold on the south bank compelled the English garrisons to the west of Orleans to retreat. Joan, clad in a coat of mail because her wound prevented her wearing plate armour, led the French out of the town to face the decamping army. She counselled caution and after glaring at each other for an hour, the English turned away. Joan had delivered the first part of her promise.

Joan's renown attracted soldiers and adventurers throughout northern France. Her presence guaranteed victory and a campaign along the north bank of the River Loire was embarked on almost immediately in June. This time, the Duke of Alençon was given supreme command by the king, but Joan's advice was to be listened to and she ranked alongside the other captains, including Dunois and La Hire. The plan was to recover the towns of Meung, Beaugency and Jargeau so as to clear a safe road for the king to

Joan of Arc arriving at Chinon to convince the French king of her mission. From a fifteenth-century German tapestry, now in the Musée Historique, Orleans.

travel to Rheims for his consecration. It was a lightning campaign in which Joan encouraged aggressive action all the time. The other captains preferred the slower, more usual pace of medieval warfare, in which negotiation and deal-making did away with the need for direct assault. At Jargeau, the French captains tried to establish a treaty of surrender with the English in which they would be allowed to leave the town in full armour. Joan vetoed

this and led the attack with scaling ladders. Inevitably, more soldiers died on both sides and the economics of such tactics may have bewildered many French noblemen, who would have liked to save lives for ransom. Within a week, the French penned in the English at Meung and Beaugency, awaiting the *coup de grâce*. An English relief army from Paris advanced to assist the

War-hammers and maces from the mid-to late-fifteenth century.

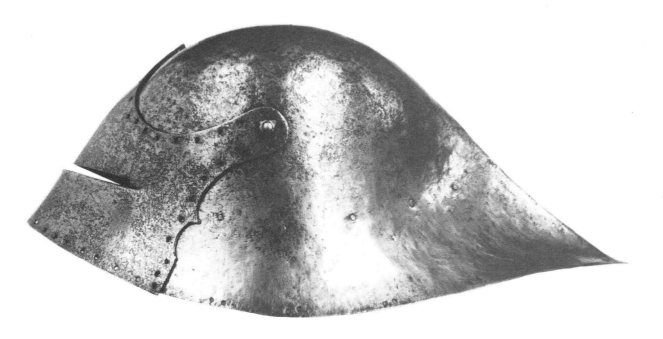

towns, but lost its nerve and retreated. 'Have good spurs,' advised Joan, ever determined to push the enemy into battle, 'we need good spurs to overtake them.' She was angry at not being allowed to lead the advance guard in its pursuit and by the time the French had overrun the English at Patay, Joan arrived too late to take part in the fighting. The road was now open to Rheims and in July 1429, Joan stood beside the king as his rule was consecrated. She had fulfilled the remaining part of her promise.

After Rheims, the brilliance of Joan's career began to wear off. The French king's political interests meant he favoured bloodless manoeuvring rather than violent confrontation. Their failure to take Paris profoundly depressed Joan and she must have felt her mission had come to an end. During the winter, her family was ennobled and she was given the surname of du Lys after the fleur-de-lys of France. In May 1430, Joan rode out to defend the town of Compiègne against a new offensive by the Duke of Burgundy. She led only a small force, without the assistance of any of the other great French captains. From Compiègne, she commanded a successful sortie against the Burgundians, but was outflanked by English reinforcements and forced to retire. Protecting her rearguard while they retreated over a bridge into Compiègne, she was forced into a field, where she was pulled from her horse by a mob of Burgundian soldiers keen not to hurt her and claim the ransom money. For 100,000 francs, Joan was handed over by the Duke of Burgundy to the English. At Rouen, she was put on trial as a heretic. The English wanted to undermine her popularity, but she conducted herself with great dignity and maintained her divine inspiration. In May 1431, Joan was burnt at the stake.

Joan's brief military career served as a model for female heroism ever after. It replaced the reality of stalwart noblewomen defending their material rights, with a new image of the inspired common woman fighting in defence of more spiritual qualities of independence and freedom. In 1472, at the siege of Beauvais, a French woman, called Jeanne Laisne, led a group of ordinary townswomen armed with axes in a sortie against the attackers. They drove them away from the town wall and captured the Burgundian standard, encouraging the Duke of Burgundy to give up his siege. She and her descendants were exempted from taxation as a reward and in annual celebrations at Beauvais, the townswomen were allowed to march before the men. She was given the sobriquet of Hachette, which like Joan's famous surname was the invention of Renaissance historians who liked to stress the Amazonian character of these warrior women, for both the bow (Arc) and the axe were typical Amazon weapons. But this classical conceit was short-lived and the abiding image of both Joan and women like Hachette is of the intuitive, amateur warrior who comes to the rescue of men when all else has failed. Over the centuries since these medieval events, this has been the preferred picture of women who take to arms. It comforts men by maintaining the difference between the sexes and by clothing the ugly violence of their real military careers with saintly or patriotic mythology. The true professionalism of ancient and medieval women warlords, who fought for land and ambition as tenaciously and effectively as their male counterparts, has been largely forgotten.

Bibliography

THIS IS, OF NECESSITY, A SELECT BIBLIOGRAPHY OF
BOTH PRIMARY AND SECONDARY SOURCES.

THE TRUE AMAZONS

Diodorus of Sicily, full history of the Amazons by a Greek in the first
century BC. Translated by C. H. Oldfather, London, 1935.

Herodotus, description of the Sarmatian Amazons and the Persian invasion
of Scythia by a Greek of the fifth century BC. Translated by A. D. Godley,
London, 1921.

Hippocrates, earliest detailed description of the Sarmatian Amazons by a
Greek of the fifth century BC. Translated by W. H. S. Jones, London,
1922.

Plutarch, *Lives*, best description of the Amazon invasion of Greece by a
Greek of the first century AD. Translated by B. Perrin, London, 1914.

Pompeius Trogus, history of the Amazons by a Roman of the first century BC
now only surviving in the work of Justin. Translated by J. S. Watson,
London, 1853.

Chernenko, E. V., *Vooruzhenie Skifov i Sarmatov*, Kiev, 1984.

Merck, M., 'The patriotic Amazonomachy and ancient Athens', *Tearing the
Veil*, edited by S. Lipshitz, pp. 95–115, London, 1978.

Rice, T. T., *The Scythians*, London, 1957.

Rohl, K. R., *Aufstand der Amazonen*, Vienna, 1982.

Rothery, G. C., *The Amazons in Antiquity and Modern Times*, London, 1910.

Samuel, P., *Amazones, guerrières et gaillardes*, Brussels, 1975.

Sulimirski, T., *The Sarmatians*, London, 1970.

von Bothmer, D., *Amazons in Greek Art*, Oxford, 1957.

AMAZONS OF THE JUNGLE

Fray Gaspar de Carvajal, narrative of the journey by Francisco de Orellana
along the Amazon by a Spanish priest travelling with him. Translated by
R. Muller, Guayaquil, Ecuador, 1937.

Cristobal d'Acuna, Inca de la Vega, and Antonio de Herrera, sixteenth- and seventeenth-century Spanish histories of expeditions along the Amazon. Translated by C. R. Markham, London, 1859.

Sir Walter Raleigh, *The Discovery of Guiana*, edited by V. T. Harlow, London, 1928.

Atteridge, A. H., 'The forest fighting in Dahomey: 1892', *Battles of the 19th Century*, A. Forbes and others, pp. 647–658, London, 1896.

Bamberger, J., 'The myth of matriarchy: why men rule in primitive society', *Women, Culture, and Society*, edited by M. Z. Rosaldo and L. Lamphere, pp. 263–280, Stanford, California, 1974.

Burton, R., *A Mission to Gelele, King of Dahome*, London, 1864.

Dalzel, A., *History of Dahomy*, London, 1793.

Duncan, J., *Travels in Western Africa*, London, 1847.

Foà, E., *Le Dahomey*, Paris, 1895.

Forbes, F. E., *Dahomey and the Dahomans*, London, 1851.

Herskovits, M. J., *Dahomey*, New York, 1938.

Skertchly, J. A., *Dahomey As It Is*, London, 1874.

Snelgrave, W., *A New Account of Some Parts of Guinea and the Slave Trade*, London, 1734.

'BRAVER THAN HER HUSBAND'

Herodotus, fullest account of Artemisia at Salamis by a Greek of the fifth century BC. Translated by A. D. Godley, London, 1922.

Historia Augusta, fourth-century collection of Roman historians chronicling Zenobia and Aurelian. Translated by D. Magie, London, 1932.

Zosimus, History of Rome, fifth-century account of the decline of the Roman Empire, including Zenobia. Anonymous translation, London, 1814.

Bivar, A. D. H., 'Cavalry Equipment and Tactics on the Euphrates Frontier', *Dumbarton Oaks Papers*, no 26, pp. 273–291, Washington, 1972.

Browning, I., *Palmyra*, London, 1979.

Colledge, M. A. R., *Art of Palmyra*, London, 1976.

Downey, G., 'Aurelian's Victory over Zenobia at Immae AD 272,' *Transactions and Proceedings of the American Philological Association*, no. 81, pp. 57–68, 1950.

Green, P., *The Year of Salamis, 480–479 BC*, London, 1979.

Wright, W., *An Account of Palmyra and Zenobia*, London, 1895.

CELTIC QUEENS

Dio Cassius, *Roman History*. Florid account of Boudica by a Greek writing at the end of the second century AD. Translated by H. B. Foster, London, 1925.

Plutarch, *Life of Marius*. Primary source for the Cimbric women, by a Greek of the first century AD. Translated by B. Perrin, London, 1920.

Tacitus, *Histories, Annals,* and *Agricola*. Accounts of both Cartimandua and Boudica by a Roman of the first century AD. Translated by A. Murphy, London, 1908.

Tain Bo Cuailnge. Irish epic poem containing the stories of Medb and Cuchulainn. Dated between the eighth and fourteenth centuries, but believed to describe a Celtic world before the coming of Christianity to Ireland. Translated by T. Kinsella, Dublin, 1969.

Feest, C., *The Art of War*, London, 1980.

Webster, G., and Dudley, D. R., *The Roman Conquest of Britain*, London, 1965.

Webster, G., *Boudica*, London, 1978.

Webster, G., *Rome against Caratacus*, London, 1981.

WOMEN OF CHRIST

Anglo-Saxon Chronicles. Only contemporary accounts of Aethelflaed and Edward to survive. Translated by G. N. Garmonsway, London, 1953.

Donizo, *Vita Mathildis celeberrimae principis Italiae*, primary twelfth-century source for the life of Matilda of Tuscany. Italian translation by F. Davoli, Turin, 1889.

Orderic Vitalis. Twelfth-century ecclesiastical history, including account of Helwise of Evreux. Translated by T. Forester, London, 1854.

William of Malmesbury, *Chronicle of English Kings*. Twelfth-century references to Aethelflaed. Translated by J. A. Giles, London, 1847.

Dornier, A. (editor), *Mercian Studies*, Leicester, New Jersey, 1977.

Duff, N., *Matilda of Tuscany*, London, 1909.

Fell, C., *Women in Anglo-Saxon England*, London, 1984.

Huddy, M. E., *Matilda, Countess of Tuscany*, London, 1905.

Kelly, A., *Eleanor of Aquitaine and the Four Kings*, London, 1952.

Kibler, W. W. (editor), *Eleanor of Aquitaine, Patron and Politician*, Austin, Texas, 1976.

Pernoud, R., *Eleanor of Aquitaine*, London, 1967.

Stafford, P., *Queens, Concubines, and Dowagers*, London, 1983.

Wainwright, F. T., 'Aethelflaed, Lady of the Mercians', *The Anglo-Saxons*, edited by P. Clemoes, pp. 53–69, London, 1959.

HUNDRED YEARS WAR WOMEN

Christine de Pisan, *The City of Ladies*. Defence of women past and present, written in 1404. Translated by B. Anslay, London, 1521.

Christine de Pisan, *The Treasure of the City of Ladies*. Practical manual for women on day-to-day survival, written in 1405. Translated by S. Lawson, Harmondsworth, 1985.

Christine de Pisan, *Feats of Arms and Chivalry*. Military manual for contemporary commanders, written in 1408. Translated by W. Caxton, London, 1490; reprinted in London, 1932.

Froissart, *Chronicles of England, France, and Spain*. Contemporary history of the Hundred Years War, including account of Countess of Montfort. Translated by T. Johnes, London, 1848.

Florent, A., *Aux Temps Heroiques de Jeanne Hachette*, Paris, 1945.

Gies, F., *Joan of Arc: The Legend and the Reality*, New York, 1981.

Jones, M., 'The Breton Civil War', *Froissart: Historian*, edited by J. J. N. Palmer, pp. 64–81, Woodbridge, Suffolk, 1981.

McLeod, E., *The Order of the Rose: The life and ideas of Christine de Pizan*, London, 1976.

Pernoud, R., *Joan of Arc: By Herself and Her Witnesses*, London, 1964.

ACKNOWLEDGEMENTS

Illustrations on pages 10, 11, 13, 17, 29, 63, 65, 69, 71, 77, 85, 103, 115 courtesy of the British Museum, London; on page 87 courtesy of the Royal Museum of Scotland, Edinburgh; all other pictures courtesy of Peter Newark's Historical Pictures, Bath.

Index

Page numbers in *italic* refer to illustrations